TEACHING
AND
LEARNING

TEACHING AND LEARNING

An Integrated Approach to Christian Education

Ronald P. Chadwick
Th.M.,Ph.D.

Fleming H. Revell Company
Old Tappan, New Jersey

Library of Congress Cataloging in Publication Data

Chadwick, Ronald P.
  Teaching and learning.

  Bibliography: p.
  1. Christian education.   I. Title.
BV1471.2.C45   207   81-19931
ISBN 0-8007-1267-6   AACR2

TO my wife, Sally, and our four sons, Randall Scott, Stephen Michael, Robert Paul, and Scott Michael. Their love, patience, sacrifice, and encouragement have been an inspiration to me.

CONTENTS

INTRODUCTION

Dr. Ronald Chadwick brings exciting credentials to the preparation of this book. An expert classroom communicator himself, he has supplemented almost two decades of teaching experience with postgraduate degrees in theology and education, enabling him to grasp both theory and practice of integration.

His classrooms have been workshops in which the principles of these chapters have been hammered out. The great psychologist Kurt Lewin once suggested that there is nothing more practical than a good theory. Yet theoretical principles must be implemented, and one of the strengths of Dr. Chadwick's work is its emphasis on "passing the torch" to student implementation.

One further thought: The integration of truth and Christian education is not for sluggards. Pedagogical lightweights will have constant struggle with a volume like this because it demands serious commitment to thinking and doing. But Hebrews 12:12 is still a part of Holy Writ, and we're all, therefore, required to "strengthen our feeble arms and weak knees" and get on with the task Dr. Chadwick has so clearly mapped out.

KENNETH O. GANGEL, PhD

INTRODUCTION

It is good for Dr. Ronald P. Chadwick to share his study, his thinking, and his life, through this vigorous book. The material is mature; it has been polished over numerous years through his teaching in the classroom, through his preaching, and through his teaching in Christian-education seminars throughout America. He writes the way he speaks: forthrightly and with conviction.

The book is a distinguished contribution to Christian education because of its content and because of its broad appeal to college students, graduate students, Christian-school teachers, administrators, and Christian-education workers in the church. It is a durable book, written with an understanding of our times. It expresses powerful ideas that have the capacity to become widely influential.

Dr. Chadwick's background as a well-trained theologian and educator enables him to write effectively both about Hebrew and Greek words in the Scriptures and of the thoughts of Dewey, Herbart, and many other educators. His blend of the philosophical and the practical is noteworthy. Sections showing the Scriptures' relevance to education are outstanding and demonstrate his commitment to the inspiration, authority, and inerrancy of the Bible.

Educational issues are raised through the technique of asking hard questions. The questions are answered reasonably, after which there are sometimes summary statements. Heavy thoughts are illuminated by good use of quotations or by allusions to the writings of others. The diagrams and the charts are plain, understandable, and add to the book's impact. It is a volume to be marked and referred to subsequently, a valuable edition in a Christian-education library.

Teaching and Learning: An Integrated Approach to Christian Education is not presented as the conclusive word on the topic. It is, however, a major work to give those who serve God in Christian education, a clarification of their mission, and shows the way it is to be accomplished. It is a benchmark. For this I thank Dr. Chadwick, a leading Christian educator. I also thank his God.

ROY W. LOWRIE, JR., EDD

PART ONE

What Is Christian Education?

1

The Distinctive Definition of Christian Education

"What is education?" "What is Christian education?" Certainly these important questions should be answered by anyone who is interested in the teaching-learning process. It is only when we understand the meaning of *education* and have an idea what Christian education is *not* that we can begin to build a positive definition of Christian education and evaluate its impact on lives.

Definitions of Education

According to John Dewey, the most familiar meaning attached to the word *education* is what goes on in a school or some other place of learning.[1] This is not a very broad definition and ignores many facets of the educational process. Covering a wider range, Dewey emphasized process when he gave this technical definition of *education:* "Reconstruction or reorganization of experience which adds to the meaning of experience, and which increases ability to direct the course of subsequent experience."[2] In the final analysis, Dewey makes the process the totality of education, in accord with his instrumental view of aims and his rejection of ultimate ends.[3]

Paul Monroe widens his definition to include both product and process:

Speaking generally, education signifies the sum total of processes by means of which a community or social group, whether small or large, transmits its acquired power and aims with a view to securing its own continuous existence and growth.[4]

Dr. William Rainey Harper, in an address to freshmen entering the University of Chicago, gave the following definition, emphasizing the product:

An educated man is a man who by the time he is twenty-five years old has a clear theory, formed in the light of human experience down the ages, of what constitutes a satisfying life, a significant life, and who by the age of thirty has a moral philosophy consonant with racial experience. If a man reaches these ages without having arrived at such a theory, such a philosophy, then no matter how many facts he has learned or how many processes he has mastered, that man is an ignoramus and a fool, unhappy, probably dangerous.[5]

Thus far it is evident that education very well takes both into account, for it may be either the product or the process of a deliberate attempt to fashion experience by the direction and control of learning.[6]

Certainly education is both the process of acquiring significant learning experiences and the product of a desired change of personality and behavior. While education may be classified as either formal or informal, the test of education is not how much one knows, but what kind of person is produced. The educational effort may be said to be woefully lacking if no observable character change is evident in the person who is supposedly involved in the educational process. To be genuine education, personal change and personality development (the product) are essential. This is achieved through the process of guided, graded experience, meaningfully involving the learner. The learner must experience change. He must grow and develop; and if he does not do so, all of the so-called educational process expended to aid him is a failure.

The etymology of the word *education* provides additional insight as to the nature of the process.

Generally, the idea obtains that the word education comes from the Latin term *educere*, which is of the third conjugation and means "to lead out." Education is thought of, therefore, in terms of drawing out the powers inherent in the person and developing them. In other words, it carries the idea of expression. The idea is good as applied to education, but unfortunately, it is not involved in the word itself. For were the word derived from the third conjugation, it would have to be "eduction" instead of "education."

Looking a little further, we find that if the word is from the first conjugation then the form is *educare*. This term, however, has a very different meaning. Instead of signifying "to lead or draw out," it means "to nourish or nurture." This carries the idea of supplying food or sustenance rather than drawing out or exercising. It is the "impressional" rather than the "expressional" idea. From this viewpoint education consists in supplying ideas or inspiration more than securing responses.

A full conception of the educational process, however, requires both ideas. First, there is an infilling process which includes the inculcation of ideas and the forming of ideals. Second, there is a drawing out aspect which includes the activity side. In other words, a complete process of education includes both impression and expression—nourishing and exercising.[7]

It may be said that all our modern education goes back to Plato. It was he who expounded an educational theory based on the principle that real education dealt with an all-around development of the body, mind and spirit of the child.[8]

Herbert Spencer said, "To prepare us for complete living is the function which education has to discharge."[9]

Today educators recognize that the goal of education is the integration of a personality within a world view. Thus, it may be concluded that education is the complete development of a personality for complete living consistent with a world view.

Education is a guided, graded process and presupposes the three essential elements of teacher, learner, and an environment in which learning may successfully take place. This guided, graded, ongoing process must assist the student in making the learning experiences his own, enabling him to develop as a person, acquiring what he needs to ultimately become an individ-

ual who is capable of achieving at his full potential. Nowhere is
character or behavioral change and vital personal development
more essential than in Christian education. The learner must ex-
hibit outwardly what has taken place inwardly. He must provide living, demonstrable proof of the power and strength of his
individual commitment. Apart from this, the processes of his experience of education have miserably failed and he certainly
cannot be said to be a genuine Christian.

The tragedy is that so many have been able to verbalize
their Christianity without ever being able to actualize it and
put it to work in flesh and blood. There is a sense in which still
today the truth of John 1:14 must become a reality in Christian
education; that is, "the Word must become flesh." Though everyone agrees that it is possible for an individual to be able to
verbalize faith in Jesus Christ and still not be truly born again,
yet as educators we continue to use memorization and verbalization to demonstrate whether or not we have achieved our
goal. One can mentally know the truth relative to salvation and
yet not be a born-again believer; it is also possible for one to be
able to verbalize how to live the Spirit-filled, Spirit-controlled
life and still not be experiencing it. The truth of Scripture is
clearly saying to us that it is important for an individual to not
only know, but also be able to do. It is a sad commentary on so
much so-called Christian education that often it produces individuals who have little else than verbalization, imitation, and
weak, inconsistent Christian living. Though education should
produce change from the outside in, Christian education is also
contrastingly endeavoring to produce change or transformation
from the inside out.

Education commonly is divided into two categories, secular and sacred (religious). However, the Christian who has
seriously thought this through cannot accept a dualistic approach to education. Reverend Theodore J. Jansma, pastor of
the Eighth Reformed Church of Grand Rapids, Michigan, indicates in his article, "What is Christian Education?"[10] that there
are at least three basic Scriptures that support not dividing
education into these two categories:

1. The earth is the Lord's, and the fulness thereof; the world, and they that dwell therein.

    Psalms 24:1

2. So God created man in his own image, in the image of God created he him. . . .

    Genesis 1:27

3. Whatever therefore ye eat, or drink, or whatsoever ye do, do all to the glory of God.

    1 Corinthians 10:31

These are not isolated passages chosen to buttress one man's ideas, but are the basis for biblical principles woven throughout Scripture and are determinative for education on the part of Christians. These principles as given by the Reverend Jansma in his article are:

1. All materials of education, every subject that may be studied, is related to God and, therefore, education cannot be divided into "secular" and "religious."
2. The person to be educated is a unified personality; he is one as God is one and, therefore, his education cannot be departmentalized into "secular" and "religious."
3. The goal of all education, in church or school, is to help man to achieve more fully the purpose of his life, viz., to know and serve God, and therefore "secular" and "religious" represents a false dualism in education.[11]

Now that a brief definition of education has been given, and it has been shown that there is a dilemma for the Christian who takes a dualistic approach of "secular" or "religious" education in isolation, I will attempt to define Christian education.

A Negative Description of Christian Education

" 'Christian education' is not an alias for 'evangelism.' "[12] It must be recognized that Christian education in the context of the Christian school is not primarily in the business of producing Christians. Though it is true especially during the elementary grades that many children are brought into vital relationships to the living Savior, the Christian school should not be regarded as the intellectual counterpart of the revival meeting. True Christian education can never really take place until the child is indwelt by the One who will "guide you into all truth" (John 16:13). Prior to this time, the child is only receiving an education in a Christian atmosphere.

Also, Christian education is not merely having a faculty or student body composed of Christians. It is just as true, however, that apart from these two prerequisites Christian education cannot exist. These, however, are not a guarantee. When Robert Louis Stevenson was informed by his wife that the maid was a good church girl, he is alleged to have replied, "Then I'd like some Christian broth."[13] Just as a church girl does not make Christian broth, so the combination of a Christian teacher and pupil does not guarantee that the education is distinctively Christian. Even compulsory attendance at chapel services or other religious exercises does not produce Christian education.

The sponsorship of the Christian school is not the deciding factor in whether or not the education is Christian. Many of the traditionally Christian colleges controlled by denominational groups have long since passed off the stage of Christian education. In some, it is because there are men and women on the faculty who cannot fulfill the first qualification of being Christians; and in others it is because they are controlled by religious indifferentists. In such cases it would be easier to attempt Christian education with a Christian faculty in a state school than it would on the campuses of these so-called Christian schools.

In addition to these, the inclusion or exclusion of any course from the school curriculum does not provide Christian education. In other words, just because the Bible is taught in a school does not make the education Christian, nor does its absence as a separate course of study make the education secular. From this it can be seen that content or subject matter does not exclusively determine whether or not a school is engaged in education that is distinctively Christian.

Based on this negative description of Christian education,

we can form a more positive approach and a clear look at what Christian education is and what makes it distinctive.

A Positive Definition of Christian Education

Paul gave a comprehensive principle of life when he wrote of the Lord, "He is before all things, and by him all things consist [hold together]" (Colossians 1:17). The Apostle John also stated an underlying principle of Christian education when he declared, "All things were made by him; and without him was not any thing made that was made" (John 1:3). Christ ought to have the preeminent place in all subject matter, since "In him are hid all the treasures of wisdom and knowledge" (Colossians 2:3). Thus, it is determined that the basis for Christian education is found in the Scriptures. It must be understood that Christian education is first a biblical discipline and so must be firmly built on a foundation of biblical theology.

Simply stated, a definition of Christian education would be as follows: Christian education deals with the process of teaching and learning (that is, the principles and practice of teaching and learning) conducted by a Christian teacher for Christians. Both teacher and pupil must be controlled by the Spirit of God, bringing all truth into living relationship with the truth of the Word of God. This is for the purpose of integrating the whole of the pupil's personality with a Word-centered, Christian, theistic world view, for the purpose of enabling man to better serve and glorify God.

Roy Zuck has provided for us a helpful definition of Christian education that though more tailored to the traditional local-church approach can be very easily adapted to Christian education in a broader context.

Evangelical Christian education is the Christ-centered, Bible-based, pupil-related process of communicating God's written Word (and all of truth) through the power of the Holy Spirit, for the purpose of leading pupils to Christ and building them up in Christ.[14]

A Christian philosophy of education emphasizing the theocentric view seeks to formulate a unified and coherent concept of God and His Word in the creation of nature and man. Thus, theistic philosophy becomes the central integrating core in the curriculum. If such be the case, the educational process should develop the complete man of God, preparing him to be completely fitted for every good work for the glory of God and the good of man. The measure of this complete man will be character like Christ's, who is the core and integrator of the totality of Christian education.[15]

This process of education will produce individuals who are not only capable of being functioning members of society, but are also capable of being functioning members of the Body of Christ (Ephesians 4:13: ". . . unto the measure of the stature of the fulness of Christ").

"For of him, and through him, and to him, are all things . . ." (Romans 11:36).

Christian education recognizes that the believer has a dual nature, in that he is made in the image of God but is a fallen creature. However, one must recognize the fact that true Christian education does not take place apart from the experiencing of the new birth by both teacher and pupil.

Real Christian education is impossible where neither teacher nor pupil is Christian . . . . The teacher may be a Christian and education may be Christian in interpretation, but unless the educand is redeemed he will not be able to think within a Christian frame of reference.[16]

The truth and interpretation of such things as the origin of life and the universe, man's accumulated knowledge, the purpose of life, and the future state are all viewed through the eyeglasses of a Word-centered, Christian, theistic world view. Because Christian education is not merely an emphasis upon teaching precepts, but rather of communicating life, it has as its goal "the perfecting of the saints, for the work of the ministry, for the edifying of the body of Christ" (Ephesians 4:12), ". . . that we may present every man perfect [complete] in Christ Jesus" (Colossians 1:28), in order that "we may grow into Him in all respects" (author's translation of Ephesians 4:15).

2

The Distinctive Philosophy of Teaching-Learning

All the history of education can be plotted on a single continuum with two extremes. On the one hand you have Johann Friedrich Herbart, with an emphasis on content, while on the other you have the extreme of John Dewey, with an emphasis on experience. To put this into more contemporary thinking, Herbart would see the teacher as primarily a disseminator of information, while John Dewey believed the teacher to be primarily a facilitator of learning.

Which is more important: the process of becoming an educated man, or the product of actually being educated? This is the dilemma that the history of education provides for us when we attempt to develop our philosophy of teaching-learning. Though the Latin root of the word *education* contains the concept both of an infilling process as well as a drawing out process (the emphasis on impression and expression, nourishing and exercising), apparently educators through the centuries have not fully accepted this. In addition, there has not always been agreement as to the necessity of balance in relationship to content and experience, the impression and expression; nor has there been agreement as to the logical order of these two elements.

From a biblical perspective the Word of God seems to say to us that impression minus expression leads to depression. In other words, the Bible tells us that the imparting of the truth minus the receipt and expression of it leads to spiritual depression. Many would say that if we are teaching the Bible, then we are teaching the right thing, and it really doesn't make any difference how we give it out. I have had people tell me that to qualify as a teacher, you only need a knowledge of your subject matter and an enthusiasm in actually presenting it. I certainly believe that these two are very essential, but apparently these alone do not fulfill the criteria that the Word of God gives to us regarding effective teaching and learning.

I do believe that it is possible to do the right thing, but in the wrong way. There are always those who respond and say, "But don't you believe Isaiah 55:11?" Yes, I believe Isaiah 55:11, but not the way most people apply it. So many use that verse as a cop-out, thinking that all they have to do is somehow spray the Word of God at people and it will not return void. If that be the case, then it would be much better for us to buy "gospel blimps" or to engage in some sort of mass saturation of areas through radio or television to get the Word of God out to people as quickly as possible. However, just as the cults so often do with verses, we have taken verse 11 completely out of the context of Isaiah 55. Isaiah begins by saying, if you are thirsty and you are hungry, and you don't have any money, come, buy and eat. In verse 2 he talks about "hearkening diligently unto me [the Lord]," while in verse 3 he talks about inclining "your ear, and come unto me: hear, and your soul shall live. . . ." In verse 6 he talks about "Seek ye the Lord while he may be found, call ye upon him while he is near." In verse 7 he says, "Let the wicked forsake his way, and the unrighteous man his thoughts: and let him return unto the Lord. . . ." Then in verses 8 and 9 he gives the words that are so often quoted: "For my thoughts are not your thoughts, neither are your ways my ways, saith the Lord. For as the heavens are higher than the earth, so are my ways higher than your ways, and my thoughts than your thoughts." These verses give us the context for verse 11. Now Isaiah says, "So shall my word be that goeth forth out of my mouth: it shall not return unto me void, but it shall accomplish that which I please, and it shall prosper in the thing whereto I sent it."

Isaiah was never implying that all we needed to do was to somehow get the Word out so that people could hear it, and then it would not return void. He is saying that as we teach and present the Word of God, we must strive to make people hungry, thirsty, and willing to seek the Lord, willing to incline their ears unto the Lord, and willing to forsake their wicked ways by creating the appropriate climate or atmosphere which enables the Word of God to be used in lives and bring about positive results. I do not believe that Isaiah had any thought in mind of the Word of God not returning void in the sense that it was drawing people either to the Lord or driving people away from the Lord. The negative was not in the mind of the writer when he gave to us Isaiah 55:11.

Some time ago someone tried to explain Isaiah 55:11 by comparing it to the miracle that our Lord performed at the marriage feast at Cana. Hiding God's Word in our minds or in our hearts was like pouring water into empty water jugs. As the water was miraculously turned into wine by our Lord, likewise when the Word of God enters the mind the Lord miraculously changes it and causes the student to grasp and understand it, as well as making it a part of his life. This really is an interesting analogy, but unfortunately it does not hold water in relationship to what the Word of God is saying to us about teaching-learning.

One of the first places we can go to for enlightenment on this is the writings of the Apostle Paul. As we consider contemporary ideas of infilling, drawing out; impression, expression; nourishing, exercising; content, experience; product, process, we discover that basically all of Paul's New Testament epistles followed the basic pattern of true education. In the book of Romans the first eight chapters emphasize the content and give us the doctrine we need to know. Chapters 9–11 deal with the dispensational aspect of the book in relationship to Israel's past, present and future, while subsequent chapters take the doctrinal truth of the first part of the book and apply it to practical Christian living. The book of Galatians—the first two chapters being personal, 3 and 4 being doctrinal, and 5 and 6 being practical—again basically follows this same pattern. Colossians, with its four chapters, also follows this pattern, with the first two chapters being more doctrinal, the emphasis being on content, while chapters 3 and 4 deal with practical instructions, emphasizing the experience aspect.

Ephesians is probably the most outstanding example of Paul's educational approach, with the first three chapters giving the believer's exalted position (seated with Christ in the heavenlies), while chapters 4–6 emphasize the practical outworking of this in terms of Christian living or experience. In 4:1 Paul says, "I . . . beseech you that ye walk worthy of the vocation wherewith ye are called." We see from Paul's use of the Greek word *axios* that we should be walking in a manner that is in balance or equal weight with the position that we have with Christ in the heavenlies. In the first three chapters, Paul uses the word *walk* only twice (both times in chapter 2). The first time (2:2) he talks about our former walk, the way we used to walk before we came to know Jesus Christ as Savior. In verse 10 Paul talks about being ". . . created in Christ Jesus unto good works, which God hath before ordained that we should walk in them." This focuses on the way we should be walking (future). It is interesting that the emphasis on walking in the present is not found until we get to Ephesians 4:1. (One commentator says that the words that describe the book of Ephesians are *sit, walk,* and *stand.* Not only is that impossible—it is illogical and does not follow the pattern that Paul has given to us.) The Apostle Paul says that first of all you need to understand that you are *seated* in the heavenlies, and then you need to learn to *stand* in this exalted position. The result of this is that you ought to be able to effectively walk in relationship to the Christian life.

Even in Paul's epistles we have given to us the logical order or pattern we need. First of all, the truth of the Word of God must be effectively taught not only in the sense that the person is able to grasp or understand it, but there must also be an emphasis on the practical application or outworking of this in terms of our daily Christian walk. The Apostle Paul is saying that it is first of all impression and then expression, nourishing and then exercising, biblical content and then biblical living. To put it still another way, the written word must be presented to the individual so that it might become the living Word in the individual's life.

A second major area we want to examine is the biblical words for teaching and learning found in both the Old and New Testaments. All twenty-five of these words, eleven found in the Old Testament (Hebrew) and fourteen found in the New Testament (Greek), are listed for your study in Appendix B. I will simply examine a few of the words, giving insights in relationship to teaching-learning theory. Then we will summarize all twenty-five of these by looking at the words themselves, the key verse(s), the key word to summarize it, and the key concept for the teaching process as well as the learning process.

The most common word for teaching and learning in the Old Testament is *lamath*. *Lamath* does not mean a mere dumping of facts or information onto the subject, but to stimulate the student to be able to imitate or apply in his life action which he has come to know. This kind of learning means to become experienced in the sense that a person becomes accustomed to something and subjectively assimilates it into his life. The word is found in Deuteronomy 5:1, where Moses talks about hearing ". . . the statutes and judgments which I speak in your ears this day, that ye may learn them, and keep, and do them." Earlier in Deuteronomy (4:10) Moses reminded the children of Israel how the Lord told him to gather the people together, ". . . and I will make them hear my words, that they may learn to fear me all the days that they shall live upon the earth, and that they may teach their children." An interesting concept that comes up continually through the book of Deuteronomy, and probably is best seen in Deuteronomy 6:1–3, is that Moses emphasized to the children of Israel that they should teach in such a way that the people would be able to observe and to do that which they had come to know.

A very familiar verse of Scripture that uses the Hebrew word *lamath* is Psalms 32:8: "I will instruct thee and teach thee in the way which thou shalt go; I will guide thee with mine eye." An interesting insight from verse 8 is that the instruction here is in relationship not to what they should know—that is assumed—but in the way that they should go in terms of how they should act or specific behavior in their life. Isaiah 26:9 talks about the Lord desiring them and with His Spirit He is seeking them, ". . . for when thy judgments are in the earth, the inhabitants of the world will learn righteousness." This evidently is not just learning the concept of righteousness, but learning it to such an extent that it is assimilated into their lives so they are living what they have come to learn.

Shah-nan is a very unusual word for teaching-learning found in Deuteronomy 6:7. It is used only once in this teaching or didactic sense, but certainly used most graphically in this extremely important passage. The word means "to whet the appetite or senses for learning": "you shall sharpen your children's minds, cut deep into their understanding that they may know me . . ." (author's translation).

Didasko is the most common word for teaching-learning in the New Testament, and the focus is on the activity of teaching. This word does not leave out the content or the doctrinal truth, but focuses more on the process or the activity enabling the person to actually learn. Ephesians 4:21 uses this word: "If so be that ye have heard him, and have been taught by him, as the truth is in Jesus." It is also used in Colossians 1:28: "Whom we preach, warning every man, and teaching every man in all wisdom; that we may present every man perfect [complete] in Christ Jesus." Colossians 3:16 also uses the word *didasko:* "Let the word of Christ dwell in you richly in all wisdom; teaching and admonishing [or mind shaping] one another in psalms and hymns and spiritual songs, singing with grace in your hearts to the Lord." Here the word is used in relationship to the word of Christ that is dwelling in you, in the sense that it is permeating the whole of your life. The outworking of this will be wisdom or the practical application of knowledge. Here the *teaching* mentioned is emphasizing the process or the activity, while the word *admonishing* is another of the Greek words which focuses on the aspect of mind shaping.

An interesting note is that Colossians 3:16 talks about the Word of Christ indwelling, while Ephesians 3:17 talks about the fact that Christ dwells in you in the sense that He dwells deep down in your heart, becoming completely at home in every area or sphere of your life. Thus we see that the Word of Christ and the Person of Christ as well as the Spirit of Christ need to become controlling factors in your life.

Paideuo is the verb form of the Greek word for "child" and literally means "child training." It is also translated in the King James Version as chastened and means to give guidance, to instruct or train in the sense of child training or child raising. It also refers to the corrective or disciplinary aspect of education and in Hebrews 12 is coupled together with the extreme aspect of discipline in the word *scourging.*

Noutheteo literally means "mind shaping" and means to train by word of encouragement. It can take on the negative meaning and emphasize the warning or reproving aspect, but it is generally translated as "admonition." This word is used by Jay Adams in the development of his concept of nouthetic counseling.

Katekeo literally means "to din into the mind or the ear" and is the Greek word from which we get our English word *catechism.*

Matheteuo means "to make a disciple," and interestingly enough is used only in the Gospels and in the book of Acts. It is never found in the noun or the verb form in any of the epistles. This causes some concern for those who feel that there is too much emphasis on discipling today, but I think the answer is simply that the Gospels and the book of Acts emphasize the purpose that God had in mind, while the epistles describe for us the process that actually is involved in making disciples.

Paratithemi means "to put something before someone" in the sense that they are able to mentally grasp it, while *ektithemi* means "to set forth, expound, or explain the facts in logical order." *Suniami* means "to comprehend or gain insight" by putting the facts together, so that they can be useful. A key passage is Ephesians 5:17, where Paul tells the Ephesian believers not to be mindless or stupid, but to understand or synthesize the will of God. This is done when the biblical facts as well as the information from the circumstances are put together and in so doing you arrive at an understanding of God's will for your life.

Hodegeo means "to lead, guide or cause someone to discover practical doctrinal truth." This is the word that is used in John 16:13 when Jesus tells us that He is not going to leave us as orphans, but He will send the Comforter, the One who is called alongside of us to lead or guide us into an understanding of spiritual truth. In Acts 8 when Philip comes and *joins* (literally, *fastens* or *glues*) himself to the chariot and hears the eunuch reading from Isaiah, he asks if he understands what he is reading. The response of the eunuch is, "How can I, except some man should guide me?" Apparently the Scripture is showing us that in the teaching-learning process there is of necessity the leading, guiding ministry not only of the divine teacher—the Holy Spirit—but also the human instrumentality.

Take a look at a summary list of all twenty-five words focusing on the key word and the key concept for the teaching process as well as the learning process (*see* pp. 32, 33).

Educators generally are in agreement that teachers teach as they were taught. The Scripture gives to us some interesting insight along these lines in Luke 6:39, 40 as well as in Matthew 10:24, 25. The Luke 6 passage literally translated says, "Can one blind person guide another; shall they not both fall into the ditch? A disciple is not above his teacher, but everyone having been perfected will be as his teacher" (author's translation). The word for "perfected" is the same as is found in Ephesians 4:12 and literally means "to equip a person." It is also used to describe the mending of a broken net, a doctor setting broken bones, or the complete outfitting of a ship in preparation for a long voyage. The Scripture is saying that as the teacher is, so the student will become.

Are there any specific passages of Scripture that can provide for us the steps, or the model as it were, that would be involved in the teaching-learning process? Certainly Deuteronomy 6 puts the emphasis on teaching in such a way that people can act upon what they have been taught. Moses outlines the steps involved in ultimately producing the desired result— namely, the Word of God becoming the controlling factor in the actions, attitudes, private and public life of the individual. Matthew 28 and the words of our Lord emphasize that teaching should be done in such a way that the people might observe the teachings that they have come to know.

Probably 1 Thessalonians 1 is one of the most complete passages dealing with the subject of the model teacher and model teaching. It provides for us some valuable insights. In verse 2 Paul emphasizes necessary preparation (". . . making mention of you in our prayers"). In verse 5 he adds that the gospel came "not unto you in word only, but also in power, and in the Holy Ghost, and in much assurance; as ye know what manner of men we were among you for your sake." Then Paul says the Thessalonian believers became followers (literally, *imitators*) of him and, as a result, of the Lord, and ". . . received the word in much affliction, with joy of the Holy Ghost" (v. 7). The result of this is seen in verses 7 and 8, where he says they became "ensamples" (literally "a model, example or pattern") to all the believers in Macedonia and Achaia. ". . . But also in every place your faith to God-ward is spread abroad; so that we need not to speak any thing." Apparently Paul is emphasizing that we must be concerned not only with the content that is being taught, but *how* it is taught, as well as the life of the individual who is actually doing the teaching.

Colossians 1:9, 10 provides for us the clearest step-by-step

Bible Words for the Teaching-Learning Process

Word	Key Verse	Key Word	Teaching Process	Learning Process
LAMATH	Deut. 5:1 Deut. 31:13	assimilating	not dumping information, but stimulating to imitation	create a response in action, become experienced, assimilation
BE-EN	Neh. 8:7, 8 Dan. 9:23	discriminating	distinguish, draw conclusions, explain alternatives	understand, so as to apply truth learned
ALAPH	Prov. 22:25	cleaving	to adopt, to hold to truth by experience	make familiar, to hold or adopt as one's own
YAH-DAG	Exodus 10:2 Josh. 23:14	observing	to know by experience	learn by one's own observation
DAH-VAR	Jer. 28:16	proclaiming	speak, say, proclaim	simply learning
YAH-RAH	1 Sam. 12:23	directing	to direct by words, example	directive learning
ZA-HAR	Psalms 19:11	warning	to illuminate the mind, instruction, warning	replacing darkness with light, ignorance with knowledge
CHAH-CHAM	Prov. 8:33	application	to apply instruction to practical needs of life	personal application of principles in daily life
SAH-CHAL	1 Sam. 18:30	attention	to become skilled in a subject through careful consideration	to look at attentively and gain insight
SHAH-NAN	Deut. 6:7	sharpening skills	to whet the appetite, to make a deep impression	gaining a deep understanding
RAH-AH	Prov. 6:6	observing carefully	see a need and make provision, provide example and illustration	learn by observation
DIDASKO	Eph. 4:21 2 Tim. 2:2	involving activity	the activity of teaching	ability to teach others also

Greek	Reference	Gerund	Meaning	Result
PAIDEUO	Eph. 6:4	instructing	guiding by instruction and discipline	growing in maturity
NOUTHETEO	Col. 1:28	mind shaping	shaping the mind by encouragement, reproof	renewed thoughts and attitudes
KATEKEO	Rom. 2:18	communicating	to din into the mind, oral communication of fact	repetition (catechism), recitation
MATHETEUO	Matt. 28:19	discipling	instruction in loyalty and devotion to a person and his beliefs	a follower who is a learner
OIKODOMEO	1 Cor. 8:1	edifying	promote growth and maturity, learning through love	maturity
MANTHANO	Matt. 11:29	experiencing	provide pattern, practice and experience	personally appropriate in personal experience
PARATITHEMI EKTITHEMI	1 Tim. 1:18 Acts 11:4	comprehending expounding	set forth clearly and plainly to present facts in logical order, explain, expound	to mentally grasp recital of facts
DIERMENEUO	Luke 24:27	interpreting	to interpret, unfold, open up, translate spiritual truth	discovery through explanation
DIANOIGO	Luke 24:31	opening	to open minds and hearts to spiritual truth	the opening of ears, eyes and heart to spiritual understanding
SUNIAMI	Eph. 5:17	understanding	to put together so as to understand	assimilate so as to apply facts
HODEGEO	Acts 8:31	guiding	cause to discover practical truth, to guide or lead to understanding	understand so as to apply truth
ANANGELLO	John 16:13	proclaiming	to dispense factual truth, proclaim, report, declare	to verbally respond

biblical model for teaching-learning. The first thing that Paul stresses is the *recognition of need* in relationship to the people he is going to be teaching. "For this cause we also, since the day we heard it, do not cease to pray for you. . . ." The Colossian believers did not face a serious spiritual problem. In fact, earlier in the chapter Paul gave thanks for their faith and hope and love. He was thrilled at the progress that they had made spiritually, and used this as a starting point for his teaching ministry to them, a ministry which followed his *preparation in prayer.* "We do not cease to pray for you. . . ." Though this word for "pray" is not the same word that Paul uses in 1 Thessalonians 1 and 5, the emphasis is very similar. Paul's concern for them caused him to pray without allowing long intermissions between his praying. The issue for the Apostle Paul was not, "How much time do you spend in prayer?" but rather, "How long has it been since the last time you prayed?" Prayer was not simply a specific period of time set aside every once in a while, but a characteristic of his life, especially in relationship to the people he was trying to teach.

The third thing stressed in Colossians 1 was the *information* or the *knowledge.* He desired that they might be "filled with the knowledge of his [God's] will." The word for "filled" is the same as is found in Ephesians 5:18 in relationship to the Holy Spirit; it stresses the fact that we need to be filled (that is, controlled) by the knowledge of God's will. This is not primarily an emphasis on quantity, but on a quality of life that comes as a result of our being controlled by God. The word for knowledge that Paul uses here is *epignosis* and probably relates the *oida,* or intellectual knowledge, to the subjective or the experiential level of our life.

The fourth thing Paul stressed was the *implication* of this as seen in *wisdom.* He stresses that they might be ". . . filled with the knowledge of his will in all wisdom and spiritual understanding." "Wisdom" is the practical application of the knowledge you already have, while spiritual "understanding" is the synthesis or putting together of the biblical facts to gain the insight that is necessary. It is one thing to know, for instance, that

God is immutable, that His character never changes. It is another thing to understand the implications of this and to be able to say, "Thank You, God, that You can be trusted," believing that whatever He promises He will do.

The fifth thing that Paul emphasizes involves *implementation*. Paul says we are to walk in a manner that is worthy of the Lord. First of all, this walk refers to walking around, and so emphasizes the total sphere of life. The word for "worthy," *axios*, stresses the need for a balance between what you know and what you are actually doing. In Ephesians 4:1, probably the clearest example of this word, Paul stresses that our walk should be in balance or in equal weight with our position (seated with Christ in the heavenlies).

Sixth, Paul focuses on *multiplication* or *fruit*: "being fruitful in every good work." Apparently, proper preparation and proper instruction in the Word of God will produce fruit in our lives, with the final result being seen in the seventh step of *maturation* or *growth*. Here Paul is emphasizing the idea of "increasing in the knowledge of God." Again Paul uses the word *epignosis* to stress that our developing understanding of God should result in our growing in the area of experiencing His Word in our lives.

The Apostle Paul is trying to stress for us that true learning begins with facts about God and ends with an increased knowledge of God; but the real goal is to produce godliness in our lives. True learning begins with information about God's plan and purpose and ends with the knowledge of His Person; but again the ultimate goal is to produce a "perfect" man. The Bible is trying to communicate to us the fact that learning just for the sake of learning, to amass knowledge, is not acceptable. The Bible is saying to us that true learning is for living.

This is also seen in Hebrews 5:11-14. "Concerning whom we have much to say and hard to interpret, since you have become dull in your hearings. For indeed though by this time you ought to be teachers, you have need that someone teach you again the rudiments of the beginning of the oracles of God. You have become as those having need of milk and not of solid food.

For everyone partaking of milk is without experience of the Word of righteousness, for he is an infant" (author's translation). The King James Version of verse 13 says that they were "unskillful in the word of righteousness," and this is often interpreted to mean that they did not have the ability to properly understand, interpret and teach the Word. Even though this may be involved, the true meaning of "unskillful" is that they were lacking experience in relationship to the Word of righteousness. In other words, they knew the truth, but they were not experiencing it in their daily lives.

There are at least two dangers that we face in our teaching. One is the danger of leading individuals to only verbalize their Christianity. We must recognize that verbalizing (expression) is the test or proof of teaching, but living (actualizing) is the proof of real learning. Our goal should not be to simply prepare students to verbalize their Christianity, but to actualize it in their lives on a day-to-day basis.

The second danger is to lead people to only have an experience or emotional catharsis in relationship to the Word. We must understand that the goal of Christian education as given to us in the Word is not just to come to know the truth, but to implement the truth, to become truth. Moses would say: *teach* to *observe* to *do.* Jesus would say *teach* to *observe,* while Paul would emphasize the fact that we should *teach* in order that people might be able to *walk* in a manner that is *worthy* of their calling.

Though it is true that John 1:14 refers specifically to the Person of the Lord Jesus Christ, there is a sense in which the principle of this verse must still be applied to us today. "The Word became flesh." Our educational system and approach to teaching-learning must be solidly based upon and centered in the Word, both the written Word and the living Word. Let us never forget that the ultimate test of Christian education is not just academic excellence, but rather character change and Christlikeness. In Christian education, true teaching-learning is always for the purpose of living more like Christ.

3

The Distinctive Philosophy of Christian Education

The far-reaching, constructive influence of a unifying philosophy for Christian schools can hardly be overestimated, for
the theory of philosophy propounded today produces the practice and product of tomorrow. As the educational philosophy is
interpreted, so the school teaches; as the school teaches, so the
student thinks; and as a man thinks in his heart, so is he.

However, a statement by Henry N. Wieman will illustrate
the problem faced at the outset.

The bomb that fell on Hiroshima cut history in two like a knife. Before
and after are two different worlds. That cut is more abrupt, decisive, and
revolutionary than the cut made by the star over Bethlehem.[1]

Well, is it? Christian theology has often called Christ the
center of history. Is a new center presented in the previous
statement?

This in a nutshell is the very problem faced as one formulates a philosophy of Christian education. Has the center changed? Is Jesus Christ (the living Word) the core, the center, the integrating factor of the educational philosophy to which many presently adhere? Is the written Word (the Holy Scriptures) the foundation upon which the Christian's educational philosophy will be built? Is the philosophy of education held by Christians a distinctive Christian philosophy of education, or is it merely the philosophy of education of many Christians though essentially built upon a man-made system?

When Christian schools first came into being, the common denominator or unifying factor was dissatisfaction with the public schools. However, this was only a negative unifier, and Mark Fakkema was convinced that it was necessary to have a positive purpose. Mark Fakkema's conviction, as he himself states it, is as follows:

> We need a Christian philosophy not only in order to meet a challenge that comes to us from without, but we no less need such a philosophy to meet the challenge that comes to us from within our Christian school movement. It is essential for the well-being of the many scattered Christian schools that we procure a common pattern of thought which will stabilize the movement as a whole and will make for unity of ultimate purpose.[2]

But what is an educational philosophy, and how does it become distinctive for the Christian? Dr. Simpson says, "Briefly stated, an educational philosophy is a statement of academic objectives and the means of attaining them."[3] Simpson also quotes DeBeer, who defines an educational philosophy as:

> A statement of purposes or relationships to be attained, or of the reasons or motives for activities or goals. Philosophy is man's way of evaluating his purposes to determine whether they are good.[4]

In the broadest sense of the foregoing definitions this entire volume then becomes a philosophy and not just the present chapter. This, however, is much too general. The dictionary definition for philosophy is "... an integrated and consistent personal attitude toward life or reality, or toward a certain phase of it."[5] Though Webster is not an adequate authority, this actually comes closer to a true definitive statement. The earlier definitions deal primarily with educational objectives and curriculum, or the materials and methods for attaining the desired goals or objectives. That which is obviously left out in these definitions is the foundation upon which the desired results are to be built. Finally then, a philosophy of Christian education is a statement of the essential basic principles which when put together provide the rudder to guide and govern the educational aims and the total curriculum or program.

A Christian philosophy is a Christian world view or *Weltanschauung*. To be even more definitive, it must be a Christian theistic world view. The normal or usual approach is to have the philosophy theocentric; but, as suggested by Dr. Lois E. LeBar in her book *Education That Is Christian*, that which is presented is Word centered.[6] A philosophy of education could be state centered, teacher centered, child centered, God centered, Christ centered, or Word centered. Out of a deep conviction that God never intended for us to separate the written Word from the living Word, and because of its comprehensive scope and consistency with a Christian theistic world view, a Word-centered approach is chosen.

World View—Choice, Not Chance

"Basic world-views are never demonstrated, they are chosen."[7] With every world view, no matter what it may be, the first principles must be chosen. By its very nature of being first, it cannot be proven; yet its principles provide the foundation upon which everything else is built. Regardless of which way a person turns, a choice must be made. Whether it be pantheism, skepticism, agnosticism, existentialism, atheism, or theism, the first principles cannot be rationally proven; they must be accepted by faith. For this presentation a Word-centered Christian, theistic world view has been chosen. No attempt will be made here to prove the position taken. It will only be stated.

Doubtless every Christian educator has some sort of philosophy underlying his views of education, but often it is an unconscious philosophy, unexpressed and unacknowledged, or at least poorly formulated. Regardless, an educational philosophy is absolutely essential: (1) to guide and govern the total teaching-learning process; (2) to effectively correlate the total educational process in the school; (3) to more wisely use the personnel, facilities and programs to achieve a more effective educational effort; and (4) to provide clear criteria for establishing the educational aims and to evaluate the educational results.

Theological Principles

Almost all Christian schools and Christian-school organizations have adopted a statement of faith. Though some of these doctrinal statements do not go far enough, they are a clear presentation of a belief in God and an adherence to the major fundamental doctrines of Scripture.

The following is a minimal statement of faith that serves as an example:

1. We believe the Bible to be verbally inspired, authoritative and inerrant in the original manuscripts (2 Tim. 3:16; 2 Pet. 1:21).
2. We believe there is one God, eternally existent in three Persons—Father, Son, and Holy Spirit (Gen. 1:1; John 10:30; John 9:24).
3. We believe in the deity of Christ:
    His virgin birth
    His sinless death
    His miracles
    His vicarious and atoning death
    His resurrection
    His personal return in power and glory
    (John 10:33; Isa. 7:14; Matt. 1:23; Luke 1:35; Heb. 4:15; Heb. 7:25; John 2:11; Eph. 1:7; Col. 1:14; John 11:25; Acts 1:11; Rev. 19:11–16).
4. We believe in the exceeding sinfulness of human nature, and therefore we believe in the absolute necessity of regeneration by the Holy Spirit for salvation (Rom. 3:19, 23; John 3:16–19; John 5:24; Eph. 2:8–10).

5. We believe in the resurrection of both the saved and the lost: they that are saved unto the resurrection of life, and they that are lost unto the resurrection of damnation (John 5:28, 29).

6. We believe in the spiritual unity of believers in our Lord Jesus Christ (Tit. 3:5; Rom. 8:9; 1 Cor. 12:12, 13; Gal. 3:26–28).

7. We believe in the present ministry of the Holy Spirit by whose indwelling the Christian is enabled to live a godly life (Eph. 5:18; Eph. 4:30; 1 Cor. 3:16; 1 Cor. 6:19, 20).

These statements of faith clearly affirm the Bible as the Word of God, the eternal triune existence of God, the creation of man, his fall and regeneration (or recreation by faith) through the finished work of Jesus Christ. Therefore, on the basis of choice, not chance or even rationalistic arguments, the position taken here is that of Christian theism, which holds the following seven basic beliefs:

(1) The Bible is the inspired, inerrant written Word of God; (2) man by nature is a sinner who needs to be reconciled to a holy God; (3) God in His love freely offers this reconciliation to all through the death and resurrection of His Son, Jesus Christ; (4) the free gift of eternal life, or reconciliation to God, is received by personal faith in Christ; (5) the basis, the integrating factor of Christian life and character, is Jesus Christ, the living Word; (6) the church, the Body of Christ, is the worldwide community of individual believers obligated to live and witness for their Lord; (7) the ministry of the Holy Spirit is not only essential in relationship to the total salvation or conversion experience, but His continual indwelling presence provides the supernatural enablement for the believer to live a godly life and be a functioning member of the Body of Christ.

United on these foundational principles, it necessarily follows that Christian education is concerned first with the individual and his relationship to God and to his fellowman. On this basis then, in order for distinctive Christian education to begin, both teacher and pupil must be vitally and dynamically related to the person of Jesus Christ, who is the living Word. This, then, becomes the essential prerequisite for the total development of the total personality in distinctive Christian education.

Basic Assumptions

One of these assumptions has already been presented, but for clarification it will be reiterated, along with two additional ones considered essential and foundational to this present work. Without a clear understanding of these basic postulates, we are left to drift aimlessly on a sea of *a priori* speculation.

Revelation. God has supernaturally revealed Himself to man through the revelation contained in the written Word. God has communicated divine truth to men, apart from which any pursuit of truth would become idle speculation and would have no validity in terms of divine, eternal truth.

Priority of revelation to reason. The Word of God is the test of all truth. When men refuse to yield to the authority of the Scriptures, they are faced with the option of complete trust in the ability of human reason. But because of the fallible and finite nature of man, human reason can never be considered as a sufficient and independent criterion. When the infinite, infallible God has spoken on a subject, there is nothing left for man to say.

All truth is God's truth. Although there usually exists a dualistic concept of sacred and secular truth, it is here assumed that all truth is from the hand of God and is intended for man's use. God is the source, the *quelle* of all truth that ever was, or is, or yet will be. A distinction still must be observed between revealed truth as declared by God and mundane truth as discovered by man, for man's relationship to his Creator is dependent upon the revelation of God in the Scriptures and not mundane or discovered truth. However, assuming that all truth is the product of the mind of God, it must be subject to and evaluated in the light of the absolute criterion for determining truth. This absolute has been given in the form of the written Word, God's written revelation of Himself to man.

Finally then, what is the scope of an adequate personal philosophy of Christian education? What are the major loci or components that must be considered as one attempts to formulate a statement of his personal philosophy of Christian education?

Authority	1. The basic foundational presuppositions or assumptions upon which the whole educational philosophy will be built: Bibliology—Bible Theology—God Anthropology—Man Pneumatology—Holy Spirit Ecclesiology—Church Metaphysics—First Principles Epistemology—Knowledge Axiology—Values
Teacher	2. The place of the teacher (education) in relationship to the potential learner.
Pupil	3. The persons toward whom the educational activities are directed.
Teaching-Learning Process	4. The process (psychology) of how persons involved in educational activities learn the things intended. (Basic assumptions about man and his relation to culture.)
Curriculum and Organizational Patterns	5. The identification of structures and processes the teacher (educator) can employ to aid learning (curriculum).
Objectives	6. The expected learning outcomes (product—goals and objectives).
Correlation-Integration	7. The relationship of patterns and objectives of educational activities to the rest of the life of those involved. (Development of a distinctive Christian world view thoroughly integrated with all of truth and all of life.) Correlation → Integration → Truth (biblical Truth and all other truth with life.)

A basic minimal statement of philosophy of Christian education must include at least the following seven points. Some of them could be combined, but in combination or separately they should all be dealt with thoroughly.

1. Bible — authority
        — content of the curriculum
2. Holy Spirit
3. Teacher
4. Pupil
5. Teaching process
6. Learning process
7. Desired outcomes (goals)

The following questionnaire has been developed primarily for use in interviewing prospective teachers, to determine their level of understanding of Christian philosophy of education. Even though the applicant may not respond with the answer thought to be best, this should provide an excellent opportunity to discuss more fully the individual's grasp of Christian philosophy of education.

It should also be noted that this teacher-interview questionnaire could be used as a review of the entire Christian philosophy of education as presented in this volume.

Developing Your Personal Philosophy of Christian Education

Teacher Interview

Part I Multiple Choice

1. Which is important in education? a) the process of education b) the product of education c) both of these d) no one can be sure.
2. Christian education is the complete development of a personality for complete living within the framework of a) a secular world view b) a thoroughly biblical world view c) an educational world view d) a philosophical world view.
3. The etymology of the word *education* shows the idea of a) impression and expression b) nourishing and exercising c) both of these d) don't know.

4. A full conception of the education process requires a) an infilling process b) a drawing out process c) both of these d) neither of these.

5. Christian education is not necessarily a) the addition of a Bible course b) Christian sponsorship c) an alias for "evangelism" d) all of these.

6. The definition of Christian education should contain the following distinctive concepts: a) Christian teachers b) Christian pupils c) control of the Holy Spirit d) all of these.

7. The final test of all truth is a) reason b) society c) the supernaturally revealed Word of God d) experience.

8. The primary role of the teacher is to be a) an investigator b) a motivator (stimulator) c) an information-giver d) none of these.

9. The primary role of the student is to be a) a motivator b) an investigator c) a good listener d) all of these.

10. Educational philosophy is a) always b) sometimes c) never d) usually involved in determining educational methodology.

11. Everything that is done by Christian educators must be measured by a) spiritual excellence b) educational excellence c) both of these d) doesn't matter.

12. Christian schoolteachers should be highly qualified individuals, but in addition should evidence the spiritual gift of teaching a) always b) sometimes c) never d) only applies to Sunday-school teachers.

13. Christian education is first a a) theological (biblical) discipline b) educational discipline c) both of these d) neither of these.

Part II True or False

14. T or F The goal of many contemporary educators is "the integration of personality within a world view."

15. T or F All materials of education, every subject that may be studied, are related to God.

16. T or F Everything that is done in Christian education
     must be justified both biblically and education-
     ally.

Part III Matching—Short Answer

17. Match the following words with the correct numbers on
     the diagram.
     a. curriculum _____
     b. objectives _____ | 1 | 2 | 3 |
     c. philosophy _____

18. Use the following ten concepts in a paragraph describing
     the place of the teacher and the pupil in the teaching-
     learning process. (Use each term at least once, more if you
     like, or use any form of the word that fits your statement.
     Two or three sentences should be sufficient.)
     1. teacher   6. real life
     2. pupil   7. biblical truth
     3. involvement   8. methods or techniques
     4. motivation   9. teaching process
     5. meaningful   10. learning process

19. Good teaching involves communication or intercommuni-
     cation. Using the following diagram and list of words,
     match the proper letters with their respective parts.

                  1 → E → 2 → D → 3
                        ↑   4   ↓

     a. message _____   c. source _____
     b. receiver _____   d. feedback _____

20. Briefly discuss your personal philosophy of Christian edu-
     cation, including all of the following concepts.
     a. authority—1. Bible 2. Holy Spirit 3. church
     b. teacher
     c. pupil
     d. teaching-learning process
     e. curriculum
     f. horizontal and vertical organizational patterns
     g. objectives—desired outcomes

Part IV Integration—Short Answer

21, 22.

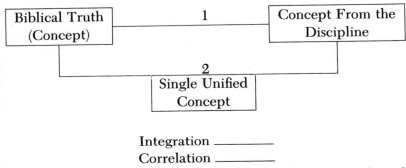

Integration _____
Correlation _____

23. Explain the statement: "Relating Truth with truth and then with life."
24. Give a statement of the biblical philosophy of teaching-learning, showing the relationship of content–experience, truth–life, knowing–doing.
25. The structure of the Bible is a) systematic theology b) biblical theology c) the books of the Bible d) there is none. Explain.
26. Explain what is meant by the structure of a discipline.
27. Explain the difference between facts and concepts and show the relationship between the two. (*See* examples *a* and *b*): a) concepts–facts b) facts–concepts.
28. Explain the statement: "All truth is God's truth."
29. Explain the statement: "The ultimate objective in Christian education is character change that is Christlike or to produce an indigenous, integrated Christian."
30. Cite an example from this last week of the Holy Spirit's ministry to integrate the truth of God's Word into your life.

N.B. All teachers must take the Taylor-Johnson Temperament Analysis and be prepared to answer questions regarding how they would handle various classroom situations.

Suggested Answers to Teacher Interview Questionnaire

Part I

1.	c	8.	b
2.	b	9.	b
3.	c	10.	a
4.	c	11.	c
5.	d	12.	a
6.	d	13.	a
7.	c		

Part II

14. T   15. T   16. T

Part III

17. a–2
    b–3
    c–1

18. Suggestions:

    a. The primary responsibility of the teacher is to motivate the pupil to become meaningfully involved in the learning process. The teaching process will be enhanced through a proper use of methods or techniques to meaningfully relate biblical truth to the pupil's real life experience.

    b. In a successful teaching process, the teacher provides meaningful motivation for pupil involvement. The learning process must relate biblical truth to real-life experience through the use of successful methods or techniques.

    c. The teaching process involves the teacher's motivation of the pupils in a meaningful learning process. To be meaningful, this process must use methods or techniques which relate biblical truth to real-life situations.

d. In his teaching process in communicating biblical truth, the teacher will facilitate the learning process for the pupil by involving the student in meaningful real-life situations using a variety of appropriate methods or techniques, thus motivating the learner in purposeful experiences that result in learned activity or doing.

e. The teacher should be a facilitator to motivate the pupil toward meaningful involvement in real-life problems using a variety of methods and techniques in the teaching process that will cause the learning process to successfully communicate biblical truth.

f. In the teaching-learning process the teacher is responsible for motivating the pupil in meaningful involvement with biblical truth through methods or techniques which utilize real-life situations.

g. The teacher relates to the pupil in the following way. The teacher should motivate the pupil, use methods and techniques which provide meaningful involvement by the pupil, and help him to discover the relevance of biblical truth to real life.

19. a–2   c–1
    b–3   d–4
20. *See* chapters 1–4.
21. Integration–2
22. Correlation–1
23. *See* chapter 4.
24. *See* chapter 2.
25. b–biblical theology.
26. *See* chapter 4.
27. *See* chapter 4.
28. *See* chapter 1.
29. *See* chapters 1, 2, 4, 6.
30. An example of the kind of answer you might receive.

Recently, the Spirit of God took a truth (cite a specific truth from the Scripture) I had come to know and because of an experience (cite the specific experience) I was encountering, He helped me to understand the truth better and to apply it specifically. It was really a time of victory and growth in the Lord.

(The incident could be a negative one where the Holy Spirit is convicting, but again the result could be victory and growth.)

PART TWO

How Is Christian Education Implemented?

4

The Distinctive Missing Ingredient: Integration

Introduction

There's an old adage in the real-estate business that real-estate valuation is dependent upon three things: location, Location, and LOCATION. I'd like to suggest a new adage for Christian education. Christian-education valuation is dependent upon three things: integration, Integration, and INTEGRATION.

What Is Integration?

What Integration Is Not!

Now that we have suggested a definition of Christian education in chapter 1, our next step is to answer the question, What is integration?

Much of Christian education in the past has been secular

education with a chocolate coating of Christianity. The morning devotion, prayer or Bible reading was to exert a hallowed influence upon the work of the day. But even the addition of a Bible course to the regular curriculum is only adding religion to an essentially secular content.

In history the word *Christian* has always referred to a world view based on the Bible. To attempt Christian education by adding a Christian frosting to the cake of man-made and man-centered philosophy is neither consistent with Christianity, nor is it distinctive. All four of the basic areas of curricular content in the elementary and secondary schools—(1) abstract science, (2) social science, (3) physical science, (4) fine arts— must be interpreted and integrated within the recognized world view, and therefore for a Christian it must be a Christian, theistic world view.

What Integration Is!

What then is integration? Probably much of what has been attempted in the past in the area of integration in Christian education has been much closer to *correlation* than *integration*. According to Webster, to *correlate* means to "have a common relation." To *correlate* is to "show a causal relationship to two things" or directly implies that two things are complementary to each other, such as husband and wife. Therefore, to take two concepts that are common to each other and to *correlate* them would simply be to show their common relationship, while to *integrate* two concepts would be to unite them together into a single unit, which possibly is expanded as a result of the two being united.

A further difference between correlation and integration is this: if bringing the two concepts together really doesn't contribute to the ongoing of the subject, then it is correlation, while integration of the two concepts would promote the ongoing of the subject, demonstrating that all truth is God's truth. Integration is the bringing together of parts into a whole, and so integration in Christian education is the living union of not only

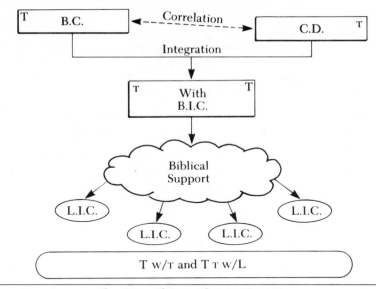

concepts with concepts, of truth with Truth, but the living union of the subject matter with life—the eternal, infinite pattern of God's written Truth woven together with all truth and all of life.[1]

Because secular education today has deliberately departed from God and His Word, it will continue to search, ever learning and yet never able to come to a knowledge of the Truth. Having turned its back upon God and His Word, secular education is powerless to put together its internal meaning. There is no integrating factor that is consistent throughout the entire system. Christian education, as Gaebelein says, is different.[2] With all its inadequacies, failures and difficulties, it has something to which to tie itself. For Christian educators, too, integration is a problem, but a problem of quite another kind than for secular education. Christian education does not need to keep looking for the integrating factor—it already has it.

The question of the center or the integrating force in edu-

Psychological Concept	Biblically Integrated Concept	Biblical Concept
	Kindergarten	
Each individual is unique and has worth and dignity		God created man in His image
	God has uniquely made each person and each person has eternal worth and dignity	
	Grade 1	
All individuals possess likenesses and differences		God has sovereignly created man as an individual personality
	God has sovereignly created man as an individual personality possessing likenesses and differences	
	Grade 2	
Each individual has special talents and strengths, and it is possible for him to develop them		God's grace has endowed all men with talents and abilities
	God's common grace has endowed all men with certain talents and abilities and His special grace equips the believer for ministry	

cation certainly is crucial. As Christians, we must see that an authoritative content and personal experience are paramount to the total development of the personality within the framework of the Christian theistic world view. The only revelation of God Himself and His Son which provides for the restoration of fellowship between Creator and creature is the written Word of God, and He never meant that the written Word should be separated from the living Word. Apart from the written Word, the living Word can never be known. Thus the concepts of a God-centered and Bible-centered approach to education are drawn together as intended by God Himself in the clearer concept of a Word-centered approach. No other integrating factor or core can match its immutability, vitality and power.

Why Is Integration Essential?

Why is the subject of integration so essential? Though it is true that education is commonly divided into two categories, "secular" and "religious," the Christian who has seriously thought this through cannot accept this dualistic approach to education, nor can he accept this dualistic approach to life.

Biblical Perspective

The Scripture is quite clear that no matter what the Christian does, it is to be done to the glory of God. The Apostle Paul in Ephesians 4 and Colossians 1 is also very explicit in stating that the goal of Christian education is to bring every man to the place of "maturity in Christ Jesus." To be *perfect* in the sense that the Scripture speaks of here is to be "complete, lacking nothing" in the sense that Jesus Christ has become completely at home in the totality of a person's life. Colossians 1:16, 17 states: "For by him were all things created, that are in heaven, and that are in earth, visible and invisible, whether they be thrones, or dominions, or principalities, or powers: all things were created by him, and for him: And he is before all things, and by him all things consist." Paul is saying specifically to us in

the last phrase in verse 17 that in Christ Jesus all things hold together. Without the Person of Jesus Christ, the living Word,
and the revelation given to us in the written Word, there is
nothing that is a satisfactory core or center or integrating factor
for an individual's life, world view, or philosophy of education.

Educational Perspective

In Christian education, we need to face the fact that when
it comes to the application of the principles upon which Christian education is built, not everybody is actually practicing
what they say they are. It is much like the old Negro spiritual—"Everbody talkin' about heaven ain't goin' there." As
Gaebelein says, "Everybody talking about Christian education
ain't doin' it."[3] Now this is not to say that we are not in any way
practicing Christian education. Nevertheless, in respect to a
thoroughgoing integration of the written Word and the living
Word, with the whole of the curriculum as well as the total administrative work of the institution, there certainly is much
room for improvement. Many Christian schools—elementary,
secondary and college level—are Christian in name only, failing to reflect Harry Blaimires' concept of the "Christian mind"
truly thoroughgoing Christian centers of education.

Professor Gordon Clark of Butler University speaks of the
Christian college where such good things as giving out tracts,
holding fervent prayer meetings, going out on gospel teams, and
opening classes with prayer are the accepted practice; yet the
actual instruction is no more Christian than a respectable secular institution's. The program is merely a pagan one with a thin
covering of Christianity; the pill, not the coating, works.[4] The
students are deceived into thinking they have received a Christian education when as a matter of fact, their training has not
been Christian and very well may not even be an education.

Christianity, far from being a Bible-department religion,
has a right to control everything that takes place in all the de-
partments within the institution. The principles of the Word of
God apply to all subjects and all areas of life and therefore, to
some extent, should alter the course of instruction. They should,

that is, if these biblical principles are consciously adopted. Every realm of knowledge, every aspect of life, and every fact of the universe find their place and their answer within the scope of Christianity. As Dr. Edwin Rian says, "The present tendency in education to add religion to the courses of study is comparable to attaching a garage to a home. What the building of knowledge needs is not a new garage but a new foundation. . . ."[5] The Word of God or a Christian, theistic world view provides this foundation, and the written Word and the living Word, the Lord Jesus Christ, provide for us in education the core or center or integrating factor which is so crucial in education.

There has been a great deal of talk about the subject of integration in Christian education, but relatively little has been written. Dr. Gaebelein's book, *The Pattern of God's Truth*, certainly stands as a monumental work in this particular area, but this book is probably the only one dealing totally with the subject at hand. I may find myself crawling out on a limb and slowly sawing it off, but as I have attempted to think through this subject I have become convinced of the necessity of looking at some specific areas of implementation. The things that I am going to suggest will in no way be exhaustive in terms of their coverage or comprehensive in the sense that I feel that these are the only factors to be considered. However, I feel that these are the five areas that we need to discover and demonstrate.

Developing a Biblical Philosophy of Teaching and Learning

If in our teaching we wish to produce behavior change, what should we try to change? And secondly, how should we try to bring about such behavior changes? These two questions are obviously related and, in fact, are two aspects of a more general question which boils down to our view of the nature of man. The Christian believes that although man was created in the image of God, he fell, and regeneration or recreation by faith in

How Is Integration Implemented?
Model for Implementing Integration

Truth With truth

All of Truth
  and All of Life

(revealed truth and mundane truth)

(product: the integrated life or the indigenous Christian)

Biblical Philosophy
  of Teaching-Learning

A Living Clear
  Observable Model

(balance of knowledge and experience)

(living example)

Biblical Theology

Discerning the
  Contemporary World

(biblical framework)

(life awareness and related-ness)

Structure of the
  Discipline

(framework for the discipline)

the finished work of the Lord Jesus Christ is an absolute necessity. Man by his nature is a sinner and needs to be reconciled to a holy God. Based upon this doctrine and other biblical or theological concepts, it would necessarily follow that Christian education must, first of all, be concerned with the individual and his relationship with God, as well as his relationship with his fellowman. It is believed, therefore, that in order for Christian education to even begin, both the teacher and the pupil must be vitally and dynamically related to the Person of Jesus Christ, the living Word. This is an absolutely essential prerequisite in order for true learning to take place. The emphasis must be on the total development of the pupil's personality in Christian education.

Both Old and New Testament terms that emphasize the teaching-learning process can be categorized under the following headings:

Learning by experience or observation. Lamath, yah-dag, rah-ah, didasko, and manthano all stress the importance of learning by involvement and observing. The student is actively involved, not simply soaking up information.

Teaching to have results. Lamath, manthano, and didasko stress the importance of telling so others can do and learn by doing. In the use of nchutheteo, the result of edification and admonition is by the promotion of spiritual encouragement. The result of teaching in the use of matheteuo is to make disciples, a definite target and goal to aim for.

Direction or instruction. The importance and proper direction and leading is emphasized in yah-rah and hodegeo; instruction by warning is expressed in za-har; instruction for practical needs is expressed in chah-cham; the disciplinary need in training and education is stressed in paideuo; the simple giving out of information is seen in katekeo; disciples are instructed in matheteuo.

Learning by drawing conclusions and understanding for usefulness. Be-en stresses the importance of the student drawing his own conclusions from an incident. Through sah-chal, a person can gain understanding on a matter if he will simply ponder or consider the situation very closely. When suniami is used, the Christian must be able to obtain understanding by putting many biblical facts together.

Mind shaping. When shah-nan is used, it shows the parent giving his child just enough information and in the right manner to influence his understanding. In the use of noutheteo, the hearers or readers were written to in order that they might be encouraged or admonished and therefore changed by the instruction.

Teaching clearly. Methods of teaching are very important and are seen first in paratithemi with the importance of teaching so the pupil can grasp the meaning; secondly, in ektithemi where the method is arranging facts in logical order; and thirdly, in *diermeneuo* where it is very important to explain or interpret the Scriptures.

Instruction for children. Verses using *shah-nan, lamath* (Deuteronomy 4:10), and *paideuo* all mention the need to instruct children as they are being raised.

Teaching of God. Dianoigo and *anangello* refer to the way God can open our understanding and reveal to the believer spiritual truth.

Scripture stresses the importance of the pupil's need to be stimulated to learn and then guided into the truth, which is so essential in teaching and learning. God did not intend, for the most part, to dump information upon us and watch us digest it any way we desired. God has purposed that we be taught in such a way that we will want to act upon His teaching. This is the same attitude teachers and parents ought to have when instructing children. Stimulation usually produces action.

In much of our teaching we have emphasized only the nourishing aspect (concepts), and we have done very little, if anything, in terms of exercising our students. As a result, at least in some cases students have come out with all of the answers to the questions that the world is not asking, and as a result they are not capable of competently exercising or applying the concepts learned. They have not been taught "to observe all things" (Matthew 28:20) that God has clearly given in His Word. Christian education requires both an emphasis on impression and expression, nourishing and exercising, the outer factors and the inner factors.

A look at the book of Romans shows that the first eight chapters are primarily doctrinal and deal with impression. They deal with factual information, doctrinal truth or concepts. But all of this has to be related practically to experience; so Paul takes the last part of the book (12–16) to practically relate doctrine to real-life experience (competence). Paul does this specifically in the book of Ephesians, as well as Galatians and Colossians, and James does this throughout the entire book. Martin Luther called the book of James the epistle of straw because of the emphasis on works. He would not allow the epistle to be included in his canon of Scriptures. But James is loaded with doctrine, and James is attempting to really take the doctrinal teaching and relate it specifically to practical real-life experiences. I am convinced that our young people today are screaming for relevancy, and I believe the Word of God is relevant.

What is needed in our approach to teaching and learning is to communicate concepts in a meaningful way, and then in applying and utilizing the skills learned, develop competency.

Developing a Biblical Theology

The second element is the necessity of developing a biblical theology. Some have tried to define biblical theology as any theology that claims to be based solely on the Bible. As Dr. Charles Ryrie says, "This popular notion makes biblical theology then that which emphasizes the revelational nature of Christianity while minimizing or ignoring rational or philosophical aspects."[6] Though such a theology may be biblical, it is not necessarily biblical theology. Biblical theology, according to Ryrie, deals systematically with the historically conditioned process of the self-revelation of God as deposited in the Bible.[7] Biblical theology pays close attention to the fact that revelation was embodied in history. First of all, biblical theology views doctrine in its historical context. Often a serious weakness of systematic theology is its failure to view doctrine in its historical context. Frequently systematic theology is that which determines the meaning of a verse or passage rather than the passage molding the system. Viewing doctrine in its historical context, therefore, is the best preventive against the misuse of the theological system. The first step after the exegesis of the text is the development of the doctrinal truths, a biblical theology. The second step is the arrangement of these into a system.

Secondly, biblical theology emphasizes theological structure or concepts and provides for us the basic doctrinal threads that hold all the Bible together. Biblical theology relieves the situation where fundamental doctrines of the faith seem to be so dependent on the testimony of a few isolated proof texts.

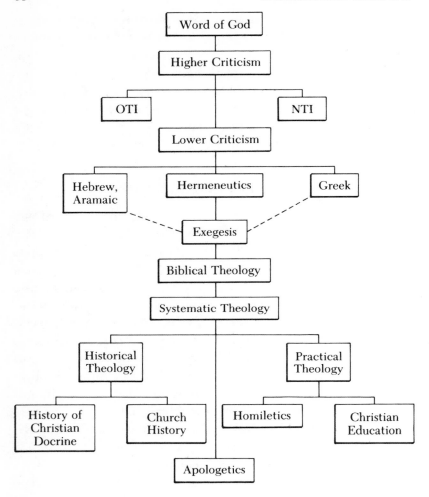

Often in the presentation of certain doctrines in systematic theology, the impression is given that these doctrines depend on only one or two biblical texts. The doctrine of inspiration is a good example. Usually two texts are set forth as the New Testament proof of this doctrine: 2 Timothy 3:16 and 2 Peter 1:21. The impression is sometimes left with the student that these are the only two texts that can be used to demonstrate the inspiration of the Scriptures. Ryrie points out that there is no better corrective for such a misconception than a study of the book of

James from the viewpoint of biblical theology. Although James does not make any direct statements concerning inspiration, an investigation of the doctrine of the Word in his epistle reveals beyond any shadow of doubt that there was in his mind a definite substructure of the doctrines of the inspiration and authority of the Word. Ryrie goes on to state that theological structure or substructure is just as valid proof of any doctrine as explicit statements, and no discipline in all the realm of theological studies reveals theological substructure as biblical theology does.[8] The structure or doctrinal concepts that hold the Bible together are probably fewer than fifteen.

1. The Structure of Systematic Theology
    a. Bibliology—The Bible
    b. Theology Proper—God
    c. Soteriology—Salvation
    d. Angelology—Angels
    e. Anthropology—Man
    f. Harmartiology—Sin
    g. Ecclesiology—The church
    h. Eschatology—Last things (Prophecy)
    i. Christology—Christ
    j. Pneumatology—Holy Spirit
2. Doctrinal Summary
    a. Angels
    b. Anthropology
    c. Bibliology
    d. Christology
    e. Covenants
    f. Dispensations
    g. Ecclesiology
    h. Eschatology
    i. God
    j. Holy Spirit
    k. Inspiration
    l. Regeneration
    m. Sin

3. Paul's Theology
   a. The Doctrine of God
   b. Christology—Jesus Christ
   c. The Holy Spirit
   d. Sin
   e. Salvation
   f. The church
   g. The Christian life
   h. Eschatology—Future things

One further aspect of biblical theology, according to Ryrie, is that it fosters a deep appreciation of the grace of God.[9] When one studies, for instance, the theology of the Pentateuch and then Pauline theology, he cannot help being impressed with the sharp contrast in the content of revelation. This is true, of course, only if in the study of the theology of the Pentateuch one is careful not to read the New Testament back into the Old. If that is not done, one can only stand in amazement at the fullness of the revelation of the grace of God in Jesus Christ in contrast to that which was revealed in the shadows of the Old Testament. Such a contrast can only bring thankfulness and humility to the heart of the one who lives today, and this awareness ought to not only give him a deeper appreciation of the grace of God, but foster within him a desire to demonstrate the grace of God in a balanced Christian life.

Discovering the Structure of a Discipline

Thirdly, there is the necessity of discovering the structure of a discipline. We have already talked about structures or substructures as they relate to theology. There is much talk today in the field of education about the structure of a discipline. But what do we mean by this? The structure of a discipline consists at least in part of the body of imposed conceptions (concepts) which define the investigated subject matter of that discipline and control its inquiry. The structure of any discipline is composed of the basic concepts or principles without which you would not have that discipline or which, when put together, form the basic, unchanging framework for that discipline. As Frank Ryan asserts in his book *Exemplars for the New Social Studies,* one-half of what the student is learning today will be obsolete in ten years, and one-half of what he needs to know in ten years has not yet been discovered.[10] This, of course, relates to factual information.

Ryan, along with others, would insist on studying a particular subject from the standpoint of its basic structure so that as new information becomes available and as older ideas become obsolete, they can more readily fit into the structure of the discipline being studied. Ralph Tyler states that the structure of a discipline deals with five basic areas: (1) the questions it deals with; (2) the kind of answers it seeks; (3) the concepts it uses to analyze the field; (4) the methods it uses to obtain data; and (5) the way it organizes its inquiries and findings. This, he says, becomes the means of analyzing the structure of a particular discipline.

Some years ago in a report of the Social Studies Curriculum Committee of the Dalton Schools in New York City, there was developed a list of common elements of the social-studies curriculum which they felt could serve as the thread running through the nursery, primary, middle school, and high school to provide the basis for continuity, sequence, and integration in the curriculum. They felt that determining such elements would serve as threads that could be used to weave a more integrated curriculum. The concept of interdependence, they felt, had implications in fields in addition to social studies—art, science, English, physical education, and so on. The value of "the dignity of the worth of every human being" is also a value to be given consideration in other subjects. Thus, these elements can be considered by teachers in other fields as possible threads for weaving a more closely integrated, total school experience, as well as serving to give continuity and sequence, year after year, to the student's experience in the social studies.

The committee went on to urge each member of the faculty to examine the list of elements to see how they either were now or could eventually be brought into their own teaching. The committee felt that emphasis upon such common elements would improve the educational effectiveness of the school by increasing the degree of integration.[11]

Tentative List of Common Elements in the Social-Studies Curriculum

Concepts

1. Regarding individual human nature.
    1.1 There are basic human needs which individuals seek to satisfy. All human beings have certain common needs, but there is variety in their manifestation and attainment.
    1.2 The underlying motivation of a person has strong effects both on him and on others. Among the motives that have had great social consequence are:
        1.21 Struggle for survival.
        1.22 Desire to get ahead, to excel others.
        1.23 Quest for security.
        1.24 Struggle for freedom.
        1.25 Desire to attain one's ideals and aspirations for a better life.
    1.3 Much of our talk and action arises from unconscious motivation.
    1.4 Frustrations in human life have serious consequences: compulsive behavior and prejudices limit individual and social effectiveness.
    1.5 Although some individual characteristics are largely the result of inborn factors, many components of the self and individual personality are formed by experience and training.
    1.6 Human beings are almost infinitely teachable. In a sense, human nature is being changed every day.
    1.7 Ideals can be dynamic in human progress, especially when they are continuously clarified, reinterpreted, and reapplied in changing situations.

2. Regarding man and his physical environment.
   2.1 Space is an important dimension in human affairs, for location affects resources, ease of transportation and communication, and many physical conditions of living.
   2.2 Time is an important dimension in human affairs, for events have roots and consequences and developments (changes) which require time.
   2.3 Climate, land features, and natural resources have profound effects on man. Development, use, and conservation of resources strongly influence his life and future.
   2.4 Man can influence his physical environment.
3. Regarding man and his social environment.
   3.1 Man forms social institutions and organizations to satisfy his needs.
   3.2 People are interdependent.
      3.21 The distribution of world resources makes for interdependence.
      3.22 Specialization and division of labor make for interdependence.
      3.23 The limitations of individual effort make for interdependence.
      3.24 Such universal human needs as affection, need to belong to a social group, need for respect from others make for interdependence.
   3.3 Social groups develop patterns for group living, thus producing customs, cultures, civilization, and society.
   3.4 Increasing knowledge and invention produce ideas and technology that disrupt some previous social arrangements. There is social lag in making adjustments to these disrupting forces. Hence:
      3.41 Society involves both change and continuity. Both are inevitable, normal, and serve useful social ends.
      3.42 The idea of progress is not a continuous straight-line development. There are some regressions and cessations of advance.

3.43 Some far-reaching and rapid disruptions lead to revolution rather than evolution.

    3.431 Intellectual revolutions.

    3.432 Political revolutions.

    3.433 Economic revolutions (the Industrial Revolution).

3.5 An effective social group must provide both for individual needs to be satisfied and for integrated productive group activity. Hence, group organization involves problems of:

    3.51 Achieving a balance of freedom and control.

    3.52 The place and limits of compromise in dealing with conflicts of personal and social values.

    3.53 Ethical and moral standards for the individual and the group.

    3.54 The place of religions in individual and group life.

    3.55 The place of the arts.

    3.56 Democratic social groups in contrast to autocratic, aristocratic, or fascistic ones.

3.6 The organization of social groups for the production and distribution of goods and services has taken several forms and involves serious problems.

    3.61 Nomadic life.

    3.62 Agriculture and family manufactures.

    3.63 Manorial systems.

    3.64 Mercantilism.

    3.65 Capitalism.

    3.66 Socialism.

    3.67 Monopoly and oligopoly.

3.7 The organization of political units affects and is affected by economic organization. It has taken several forms and involves serious problems.

    3.71 Patriarchal clan or tribe.

    3.72 City-state.

    3.73 Feudalism.

    3.74 Ecclesiastical state.

    3.75 Nationalism and imperialism.

3.76   Democracy.

3.77   Communism.

3.78   Fascism.

3.8   Social groups can be reshaped to fulfill their functions more adequately.

Values

1.   Attitudes toward self.

1.1   Growing from self-love to self-respect; acceptance of self, realization of one's own worth.

1.2   Integrity, honesty and frankness with self; objectively critical of self.

1.3   Hopefulness for the future.

1.4   Willingness for adventure; sense of mission, of reformation, of great crusade.

1.5   Desire to make a productive contribution, not to be a parasite.

2.   Attitudes toward others.

2.1   Respect for the dignity and worth of every human being, regardless of his racial, national, economic or social status.

2.2   Cherishing variety in people, opinions, acts.

2.3   Equality of opportunity for all.

2.4   Tolerance, goodwill, kindliness.

2.5   Desire for justice for all.

3.   Attitudes toward social groups to which he belongs.

3.1   Loyalty to world society and world order.

3.2   Acceptance of social responsibility.

3.3   Willingness to submit one's problems to group study and group judgment.

3.4   Balance of integrity of individual and group participation.

3.5   Loyalty to social purposes of the group rather than undiscriminating loyalty to whatever the group does.

3.6   Willingness to work for an abundance of the good things of life for all peoples in the world.

4. Intellectual and aesthetic values.
    4.1 Love of truth, however disconcerting it may be.
    4.2 Respect for work well done, worth of socially directed effort as well as achievement.
    4.3 Freedom of thought, expression, and worship.
    4.4 Love of beauty in art, in surroundings, in the lives of people.
    4.5 Respect for reasonable procedures rather than force as the only proper and workable way of getting along together.

Skills, Abilities, and Habits

1. In analyzing problems.
2. In collecting facts and other data.
    2.1 Skill in selecting dependable sources of data.
    2.2 Ability to observe carefully and listen attentively.
    2.3 Ability to read critically.
    2.4 Ability to discriminate important from unimportant facts.
    2.5 Ability to take notes.
    2.6 Ability to read charts, graphs, tables, and maps.
3. In organizing and interpreting data.
    3.1 Skill in outlining.
    3.2 Skill in summarizing.
    3.3 Ability to make reasonable interpretations.
4. In presenting the results of study.
    4.1 Skill in writing a clear, well-organized, and interesting paper.
    4.2 Skill in presenting an oral report.
    4.3 Ability to prepare a bibliography.
    4.4 Ability to prepare charts, graphs, tables, and maps.
    4.5 Ability to write a critical book review.
5. Ability to do independent thinking.
6. Ability to analyze argument and propaganda.
7. Ability to participate effectively in group work.
8. Good work habits—planning of time, efficient use of time.

9. Ability to interpret a social situation, to recognize motives
    and needs of others.
10. Ability to foresee consequences of proposed actions.

"It should also be clear that these elements are not to be
viewed as single things, each to be a separate goal of instruction. Good teaching always involves a synthesis of several elements. The same learning experience can contribute to several
of these elements at the same time—the child may in this learning experience deepen several concepts, gain a greater concern
for certain social values, and acquire increased skill in study.
The foregoing elements are suggested threads for the weaving,
but the teaching will involve the closely woven fabric. The report will have been of value if it helps to weave a better integrated cloth."[12]

It appears then that when teachers gain an understanding
of the structure of a discipline that students learn more effectively and more efficiently the content involved, as well as its
relationship to other disciplines. The same is true from a Christian perspective. The concept from the discipline (C.D.) is related to a concept from biblical theology (B.C.). At this point,
the concept from the discipline and the biblical concept are
checked and if the C.D. complements the B.C. and is not in
conflict, they are in correlation. When the two are woven together into a single larger concept, the step of integration provides us a single biblically integrated concept (B.I.C.).

Discerning the Contemporary World

A fourth area in the implementation of integration in Christian
education is the necessity of discerning the contemporary
world. The space age dawned suddenly upon a century already
beset by two world wars, the introduction of the air age, the era
of dictatorships, the jet age, and the atomic age. These and still
further developments of the twentieth century have brought
both marvelous and yet threatening changes to our civilization.

We have certainly seen that these changes have obviously

emphasized the increasing importance of science and technology, but some observers of contemporary life, including numerous scientists, have challenged the wisdom of preoccupation with technical forces, events, and gadgets. The ability to solve the problems of human adjustment to contemporary technical development requires attention, however, to social factors. Even the marvelous computer, "the thinking machine," depends ultimately upon human beings for their programming. It is not possible that evangelical Christians today still have their heads in the sand and are not fully apprised of what is happening in the world around them. It is very possible to become so buried in biblical truth that one develops a consciousness of the world to come without realizing they are presently in a world that is desperately in need of help. It is possible to become so "heavenly minded" that we are no earthly good and, as a result of this, are not only incapable of communicating the needs of the world today but, even more tragically, are incapable of equipping our students to be able to relate biblical truth and thus to be able to minister to the needs of a world lost and without Jesus Christ.

Jonathan C. McLendon in his book, *Social Studies in Secondary Education,* makes a number of statements regarding the contemporary social world. These generalizations at least give us a broad overview of what is happening in our world today.

1. The tripling of the world's population in the past two centuries as a result of rising birth rates and generally improved nutrition and medical care has caused a population explosion.
2. A rapidly increasing population has been suggested as a cause for increased social and political problems.
3. For more than a century, a relative decline in American rural population has been accompanied by an accelerating growth in urban areas.
4. The hubbub of life in the city seems to contribute to the greater emotional strain of modern times.
5. More interpersonal relationships are involved in city life than in small towns and rural areas.

6. Industrialization and urbanization bring steadily growing amounts of leisure time to the peoples involved.
7. The continuing industrial revolution has finally brought about a super-abundant production of goods without having arranged a balancing means of abundant consumption.
8. The demand for recreational facilities created by widespread leisure time has multiplied into a chief type of enterprise in our economy.
9. The very foundations of modern civilization have been shaken by the recurrent danger and actual advent of war in the twentieth century.
10. Technology, trade, exchange problems, and tourist travel have made the world economically and culturally more interdependent.
11. The past century has witnessed tremendous shrinking of the time required for increasingly rapid means of communication.
12. The social effect of a better means of transportation has been to increase the time we spend en route to places to which we otherwise would not go.
13. Though rapid transportation and communication provides a greater number and frequency of contacts with others, many of them are limited to one-time or once-in-a-while contacts.
14. In recent times, knowledge has been accumulated and disseminated at an ever more rapid rate.
15. Whatever may be the philosophical merits of educating the masses, schools have played a key role in the dissemination of knowledge.[13]

Demonstrating a Clear, Observable Model

The final element in the process of implementing integration in Christian education is the necessity of demonstrating a clear, observable model of the reality of the Person of Jesus Christ and the feasibility of the practical implementation of the concept. Recently I have had two instances in working with students that have made me increasingly aware of the necessity of the teacher in the classroom demonstrating a clear and observable model of the reality of that which the instructor is attempting to communicate. In discussing with one student problems relative to faculty members not receiving paychecks on time and obviously facing crucial problems financially, the student responded by saying that essentially his instructor was negating everything that he had been teaching him simply by the way the instructor was reacting to an opportunity to demonstrate real faith. I have seen students become so shaken by this kind of reaction that they began to question even the feasibility of being able to live (except in a sterile hospital-type atmosphere) the truths from God's Word that many of us as Bible teachers so clearly expound. Numerous times I have discussed with students the aspect of trusting God and stepping out by faith. Often the student responds by telling me that apparently after years in a Christian school, he has not really learned what it is to trust God and be able to step out by faith.

It is interesting that a non-Christian educator such as Ralph Tyler states in connection with the problem of guiding the learner in carrying on a desired behavior that he has found that students commonly observe the teacher's behavior as a model to direct their own. He goes on to say that this is a useful guide if the teacher does frequently demonstrate the behavior the student is expected to acquire, but some teachers do not furnish an observable model of the desired learning behavior.[14] The instructor often only lectures to a class, maybe only demonstrating ways of giving out information rather than showing the student how he goes about solving problems. When students cannot gain a clear picture of what they are to do by observing the teacher, they depend upon other students to show them or tell them. Obviously, this results in frequent misunderstanding of what the student is to do. It is therefore imperative that clear, observable models be provided as a means of guiding the student to produce the desired behavior results.

As children and young people grow up, they often find individuals who seem particularly attractive and seek to emulate them. The young child may begin this process of identification with his mother, following her around the house in an attempt to imitate her behavior. During the years of development other persons, in turn, are objects of identification. This process is one of the ways in which young people learn; and with a variety of constructive personalities available, the outcome can be positive and include the acquisition of attitudes, values, and interests, as well as skills and practices. However, in some of our schools the range of constructive personalities that are close enough to the students to permit attraction and emulation is much too narrow, so that many children and young people find no one on the faculty enough like them to be drawn into identification. This is another consideration for instructional planning that should seek to use all of the important resources, especially the human resources, that can possibly be provided for learning.

The Apostle John in John 1 states that "the Word was made flesh, and dwelt among us, and we behold his glory." Essentially what John is saying is that we saw Him, we touched Him, we beheld His glory. We saw Him operate. We saw Him reflect the realities of what He spoke and saw that there was consistency not only in the words that He spoke, but in the life that He lived. What our students need to see so desperately today is a clear, observable model of the reality of Jesus Christ and a communication both by words and by life that it is absolutely feasible to live a life of faith. This is not only the integration of Truth with truth, but Truth/truth with life.

Summary

I believe that it is possible to make a few summary statements regarding this extremely crucial subject of integration in Christian education, but I certainly would make no attempt to draw conclusions. I believe that a topic such as this can never really be concluded and that I can only give a few summary statements of the thoughts that I have attempted to communicate. It appears to me that the principle that can be drawn from our brief look at the subject of integration is that learning is most effective when that which is learned is integrated with all of

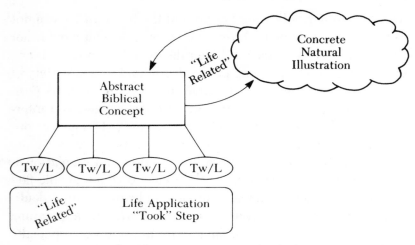

The Closer You Stay to Real Life the
More Meaningful Your
Teaching Will Be

truth and all of life. Ideally this never really ends, for even when you have taught a group to be honest, ideally it isn't completed until the individual is able to bring the concept of honesty into every area of his life. Obviously this is not learning truth in isolation, but attempting to learn truth in relationships and ultimately in integration. Things learned in one situation should not just be correlated or shown to be complementary to another situation, but they should be vitally united and in this way transferred to other areas and even to other cultural settings.

To the extent that the truths presented are integrated with the truth of the written Word and then are transformed into experience both in and out of the classroom, to this extent is maturity in Christ developed and the ultimate goal of Christian education brought to fruition. Christian-education valuation is dependent upon integration. Colossians 3:17 says, "Whatsoever ye do in word or deed, do all in the name of the Lord Jesus, giving thanks to God and the Father by him."

Summary Study Questions

1. Define correlation.
2. Define integration.
3. Explain: Truth with truth and with life.
4. What is meant by the statement "structure of the discipline"?
5. What is the structure of the Bible?
6. In integration, why and how is the teacher a model?
7. Explain the difference between facts and concepts.
8. What is concept-with-concept integration?
9. Why is contemporary awareness necessary?
10. What is meant by the indigenous or integrated Christian?

5

The Distinctive Philosophy of Curriculum

Introduction

According to the traditional approach to education as viewed in Herbart, the outer factors of the pupil are emphasized and education becomes teacher centered. In progressive education, as illustrated in the teaching of John Dewey, the inner factors are stressed, with the result that education becomes pupil centered. For years Christians have been content to buy up whatever educational ideas were prevalent at the time—from Herbart and traditionalism, to Dewey and progressivism. However, since it is true that Christian education is distinctive, then it is not legitimate to have the same integrating factor in a distinctive Christian philosophy of education as would be found in a man-made system.

Is it not sufficient to have a God-centered or Bible-centered education? Certainly if God and the Bible are not at the center, it can never be Christian. It is believed, however, that God never meant that the written Word and the living Word should be separated. The integrating factor in the individual's Christian life obviously should be the living Word, Jesus Christ, who is "the same yesterday, and today, and for ever" (Hebrews 13:8). With Jesus Christ at the center, there is a nonterminating core and all of life is integrated around a Person who never changes. But the living Word can only be known through the revelation of the written Word, which is the integrating factor in Christian education for mundane truth.

A God-centered or Bible-centered approach is not incorrect, but does not clearly show the relationship of Jesus Christ, the living Word, and the Bible, the written Word. In stating that the educational philosophy is Word centered, it is believed that this then shows the balance between the outer and inner factors, the Bible and Jesus Christ (John 1:1–4; 8:58; 10:30; Exodus 3:14).

To the extent that the truths presented are integrated with the truth of the written Word and then are transformed into experience both in and out of the classroom, to this extent is maturity in Christ developed and the ultimate goal of Christian education brought to fruition. This concept is illustrated in the following diagram by Dr. LeBar.[1]

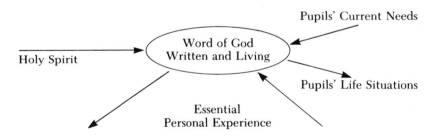

Thus, the center of Christian education, and specifically the area of curriculum, does not change with every new idea on the educational market, nor is it centered in sinful human life, but rather in the One who is divine life Himself, eternal life, fullness of life, the living Word revealed by the written Word.

It is not the book but the Person revealed in the book who gives the dynamic vitality and power needed in a distinctive Christian philosophy of curriculum.

Definition of Curriculum

The transition from a Word-centered, Christian, theistic world view to actual teaching practice is bridged by the curriculum. The word *curriculum* is derived from the Latin *currere*, which means "to run" and in ancient Rome referred to "running on a racecourse." The dictionary commonly defines *curriculum* as a "course of study . . . or a body of courses offered by an educational institution. . . ." Smith, Stanley, and Shores have described this concept of curriculum:

A sequence of potential experiences as set up by the school for the purpose of disciplining children and youth in group ways of thinking and eating . . . a set of educational objectives, a body of subject matter, a list of exercises or activities to be performed, a way of determining whether or not the objectives have been reached, a kind of control the teacher is expected to exercise over learners—these things comprise the curriculum.[2]

Whether we are referring to elementary, secondary, higher education, or church education, the curriculum may be defined narrowly as the courses offered, or broadly as all the experiences offered by the school, or the particular experiences a given student has while in school. Traditionally the course or curriculum was considered the body of content that the student covered in his educational progress. More recently, the term connotes the activities of the student as he is engaged in various experiences which involve content.[3]

In a Scriptural orientation, the "curriculum" may be defined as those activities in relation to authoritative content that are guided or employed by Christian leadership in order to bring pupils one step nearer to maturity in Christ.[4]

However, the question of the center, the integrating force, becomes crucial in structuring a curriculum. As Christians, we must see that an authoritative content and personal experience are paramount to the total development of the personality within the framework of the Christian, theistic world view.

Can Christians accomplish their aims and objectives in a curriculum that is man centered? Some have proposed that only a God-centered curriculum can be Christian; and this is absolutely correct, for without God, an atheistic world view is all that remains. However, the only revelation of God Himself and His Son which provides for the restoration of fellowship between Creator and creature is the written Word of God, and He never meant that the written Word should be separated from the living Word.

In chapter 4 on teaching-learning, as well as in chapter 3 in defining Christian education, we have seen that education must be both product and process. It is a balance of both content and experience, truth and life. Apart from the written Word (content) the living Word (experience) can never be known. Thus, the concept of a God-centered and Bible-centered approach are drawn together as intended by God Himself in the clearer concept of a Word-centered approach. No other center can compare for its immutability, vitality, and power.

In planning, carrying out, and evaluating instructional programs at any level of education, a series of basic questions must be answered.

1. What educational purposes should the school seek to attain?
2. What educational experiences can be provided that are likely to attain these purposes?
3. How can these educational experiences be effectively organized?
4. In what order or sequence shall these educational experiences be offered?
5. How shall we determine whether these purposes are being attained?
6. Who shall determine the answers to these questions?
7. By what procedure shall decisions on these questions be made?[5]

When these seven questions have been answered and the

answers implemented, the instructional program (curriculum) of the school or church has been both defined and developed.

Concept-Competence Curriculum

The Experience–Subject-Matter Curriculum in Education

Experience Curriculum	Subject-Matter Curriculum
firsthand observation—active involvement	secondhand observation—passive involvement
integrated experience	imposed experience
wholistic approach	atomistic approach
process oriented	content oriented
diversity of learning	uniformity of learning
teacher and student active	teacher active—student passive
achievement—individual scale	achievement—normative scale

Another approach to curriculum has been suggested by Lewis Mayhew, who proposes a general education based on selected experiences. Mayhew proposes that every college student should:

1. Have the opportunity to engage in independent study in which he sets his own goals and proceeds at his own rate, decides when he is finished, and feels free to use or not use professional resources of the institution.
2. Learn in large and impersonal situations.
3. Learn to function in small groups.
4. Have a relationship with an adult professional person which is sustained over a period of time.
5. Have a sustained off-campus experience of some sort.
6. Have the opportunity to know intimately a culture or sub-culture different from his own.
7. Be required to make a sustained effort over a prolonged period of time on a particular task.
8. Have the opportunity to engage in a number of brief *ad*

hoc activities which have the same curricular value as longer and more sustained efforts.

9. Enjoy, unpenalized, opportunities to engage in play for his own personal satisfaction.
10. Have opportunities to gain deeper understanding of his own emotions and those of others.
11. Have a chance to learn by using some of the newer media.
12. Have an aesthetically creative experience regardless of the level of his performance.[6]

The concept-competence curriculum, from a Christian perspective, attempts to integrate the student's cognitive development with the development of his total personality in relation to a thoroughly biblical world and life view for the purpose of producing character change that demonstrates maturity in Jesus Christ. This approach to curriculum is solidly based in and dependent upon God's revelation, but not without reasonably and rationally tying it to reality.

The Most Crucial Questions in Regard to Curriculum for the 1980s

1. What is the basic purpose or philosophy of curriculum?

   Without an adequate conception of what we mean or include in our concept of curriculum, we will lack a rudder to give us theoretical and practical direction.

2a. What is our understanding of the philosophy of teaching?

   An adequate conception of the role or function of the teacher as a motivator, stimulator, or guide to cause the student to personally become meaningfully involved in the process will greatly affect our concept of curriculum.

2b. What is our understanding of the philosophy of learning?

   The role of the student as an active rather than passive participant in the process is also vital to our approach to curriculum and the process of learning.

A Pattern for Purposeful Pedagogy
Concept-Competence Model
A Reality-Oriented Model Based Upon Revelation

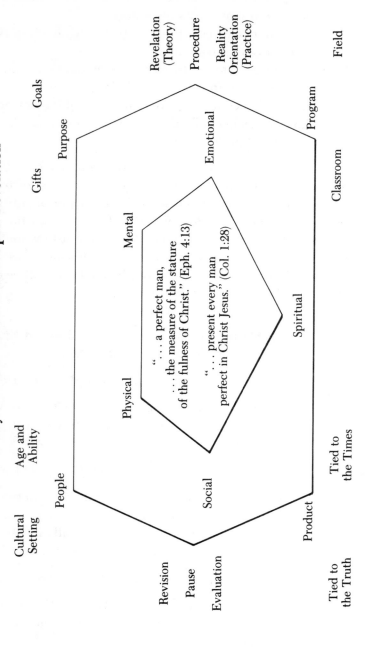

Cultural
Setting

Age and
Ability

Gifts

Goals

Purpose

People

Revelation
(Theory)

Procedure

Reality
Orientation
(Practice)

Field

Program

Classroom

Emotional

Mental

" . . . a perfect man,
. . . the measure of the stature
of the fulness of Christ." (Eph. 4:13)

" . . . present every man
perfect in Christ Jesus." (Col. 1:28)

Physical

Spiritual

Social

Product

Tied to
the Times

Revision
Pause
Evaluation

Tied to
the Truth

3. What are the "operationally defined" or behaviorally stated objectives?

    As our philosophy gives us direction, our goals tell us specifically what we are moving toward.

4. What is the basic structure of the subject or content areas to be taught? (The structure of the discipline is made up of the basic concepts which form the framework for that discipline, and that structure does not change.)

    With the rapid information explosion we can't possibly teach all the facts, but we need to give students a basic framework to which they can continually add information as it becomes available.

5. What are the relevant world, national, and community needs and problems we must be aware of?

    This will require that our curriculum planning be flexible in order to keep it fresh and relevant to meet the needs of our students.

6. What educational experiences do we want our students to have in the school classroom as well as in the community?

    Our curriculum will of necessity need to be wedded to real life and so will demand not only knowing, but applying and utilizing what the students know.

7. How will these educational experiences be organized?

    This will require careful planning of teaching strategies for learning in and out of the classroom.

8. What horizontal (classroom) and vertical (grade level) organization will be utilized?

    My recommendation would be a 4–4–4 (grades 1–4, 5–8, 9–12) vertical organization utilizing both homogeneous and heterogeneous multi-age-level groupings in an integrated or modified open-concept approach.

9. What procedures will be utilized to evaluate the degree of accomplishment of our behaviorally stated objectives?

The watchword today is accountability; so we will need to determine our successes and failures. Educational evaluation is always on the basis of educational objectives; so the clearer we have stated our objectives, the more accurately we can evaluate them.

10. By what means will we proceed to train teachers to implement in practice the theoretical model of curriculum we have established?

This undoubtedly will be our most difficult problem, unless the teacher-training institutions quickly provide for us instructors and courses where this creative, innovative model is implemented.

6

The Distinctives of the Christian School

Distinctive Problem

Nine of the first ten American colleges were distinctively Christian institutions. But the public-school system, unlike the colleges, was not so inspired.[1] On the other hand, the public schools were not intended to be irreligious, for references to God and Jesus Christ were to be found in the readers of two generations ago.

No such reference can be found in the public-school books today, and the reason is not hard to find. The public schools were founded with the idea of not favoring one Christian denomination over another or of not favoring one religion above another. The result is that they now favor no religion at all and are completely secularized.[2]

It is self-evident that on this scheme ... the United States system of national popular education will be the most efficient and widespread instrument for the propagation of Atheism which the world has ever seen.

The claim of impartiality between positions as directly contradictory as that of Jews, Mohammedans and Christians, and especially that of theists and of atheists, is evidently absurd. And no less is the claim absurd and impossible that a system of education can be indifferent on these fundamental subjects. There is no possible branch of human knowledge which is not purely formal, like abstract logic or mathematics, which can be known or taught in a spirit of entire indifference between Theism and Atheism . . . if it be not positively and confessedly theistic, it must be really and in full effect atheistic.[3] (*See* Appendix D for the Hodge lecture.)

Originally the idea was not to favor one denomination or even to attack Christianity, but to remain completely neutral. Because the majority of Protestants believed the promises of the schoolmen that they would not take the offensive against religion, the Protestants did not establish primary schools; but the Romanists did.[4] Time has proven that the Romanists adopted the wiser course, for the promises of the schoolmen were broken.

Today Christian principles are under attack in the public-school system. Reports come that the evolutionary denial of the creation of the world is being taught in second grade.[5] How can a child of seven or eight stand against an organized attack on the theistic world view? How can parents protect their children? The public school, though in reality only reflecting the general attitude of society, makes no pretense of being neutral in religious matters; and when parents here or there protest, they are promptly ridiculed and silenced. "The notion of religious liberty or even the toleration of Christianity, that is, the original claim to neutrality, is not part of the school men's mental equipment."[6]

The law of the State of Illinois forbids teachers the right to read the Bible in the classroom, but teachers may deny creation by God and denounce Christianity there.[7] Though the irreligious have seized the right to exclude Christianity, Christians are denied the right to exclude attacks on Christianity, making the promise of neutrality a farce.[8]

Philosophy, ethics, jurisprudence, political and social science can be conceived of and treated only from a theistic or from an atheistic point of view. The proposal to treat them from a neutral point of view is ignorant and absurd.[9]

It is not sufficient to say that the deficiency of the national system of public-school education will be adequately supplied by the activities of the Christian churches. The child spends only 1 percent of his time at church, while he spends 16 percent of his time in school and the remaining 83 percent of his time at home.

No court would admit in excuse for the diffusion of poison the plea that the poisoner knew of another agent actively employed in diffusing an antidote. Moreover, the churches, divided and without national recognition, would be able very inadequately to counteract the deadly evil done by the public schools of the State with all the resources and prestige of the government.[10]

To say that man can be educated for good citizenship or for this or that position without religion "is as unscientific and unphilosophical as it is irreligious."[11] This view deliberately leaves out the proposition that man is essentially just as religious as he is rational.

In the February 27, 1961, issue of *Christianity Today*, T. Robert Ingram, Rector of St. Thomas School in Houston, conclusively showed in his article that education and faith, notwithstanding the objections of some, cannot be separated. Mr. Ingram feels that the present-day educational system demonstrates the reality of the statement by Professor Hodge concerning national education separated from religion. The very constitution of the state school system poses a very serious dilemma for Christian parents, for "teaching and learning based upon Christian faith and Christian scholarship are ruled out."[12]

In 1961 the Rural Bible Mission of the United States was stripped of its Bible-teaching program in the thirty-one counties of Michigan, all because four parents of elementary pupils near Williamston asked the State to compel the Mission to end its instruction program in the local school.[13] It does seem strange that four godless parents could override the desire of thousands of parents who would vote for the Bible's supreme place and value in educating well-behaved and God-fearing boys and girls.

Obviously the public schools are not Christian, and there is no pretense at neutrality, for the Bible is prohibited. In 1962, while teaching in a public school in Colorado, I was warned that the Bible that was on my desk had to remain a closed book from the time school started until the time school was out. The superintendent warned that I dare not make the law a test case in that school district. Christian parents for years have been duped into believing that the public-school position is one of neutrality.

The tendency is to hold that this system must be altogether secular. . . . It is capable of exact demonstration that if every party in the state has the right of excluding from the public schools whatever he does not believe to be true, then he that believes most must give way to him that believes least, and then he that believes least must give way to him that believes absolutely nothing, no matter in how small a minority the atheists or the agnostics may be. It is self-evident that on this scheme, if it is consistently and persistently carried out in all parts of the country, the United States system of national popular education will be the most efficient and widespread instrument for the propagation of Atheism which the world has ever seen.[14]

"The fear of the Lord is the beginning of knowledge" (Psalms 111:10) but the public schools give the pupils the notion that knowledge can be had apart from God. The prayer of many who teach in the system of public education is well expressed by Clark when he says, "O God, we neither deny nor assert Thy existence and, O God, we neither obey nor disobey Thy commands; we are strictly neutral."[15]

For unthinking Christians, this may sound fair enough; however, teaching is accomplished by exclusion as much as by inclusion, by omission as much as by emphasis. The school system that ignores God teaches its pupils to ignore God. "If God be banned from the public schools, those who ban Him must accept the responsibility for the entrance of the devil."[16]

Distinctive Purpose

Over eighty-five years ago Professor Hodge of Princeton said:

I am as sure as I am of the fact of Christ's reign that a comprehensive and centralized system of national education separated from religion, as is now commonly proposed, will prove the most appalling enginery for the propagation of anti-Christian and atheistic unbelief ... which this sin-rent world has ever seen.[17]

The purpose of Christian education is to provide a distinctive education for the Christian life, with the result that the person can better serve and glorify God. A good education should equip a person to be a functioning member of society. A good *Christian* education should equip a person to be a functioning member of society, but also a functioning member of the Body of Christ. With this statement of purpose, it is seen that secular or public-school education and Christian education are diametrically opposed. There is a vast difference between the Christian and the non-Christian viewpoint of any given subject. This is true because subjects can never be taught in a vacuum. The whole context of one's life will have a bearing on the presentation of any given subject. Thus, even though knowledge is factually the same for believer and unbeliever, no subject can be taught in the totality of its truth if its originator is ignored. "For Christian education to adopt as its unifying principle Christ and the Bible means nothing short of the recognition that all truth is God's truth."[18]

Distinctive Product

It has previously been stated that education is both product and process, impression and expression, content and experience, nourishing and exercising. When one begins a study of the product of education, it must deal with a study of the aims or objectives of the process. The problem, however, is that even though on the surface the result or product might appear to be the same, there is little consensus as to the purpose or objective toward which the process was aimed. The following illustrates this situation.

Ever since the first adult began to pass on his knowledge to his or to other people's children, there has probably been more or less discussion as to what the training was really for. Such primitive groups as still exist show a diversity in their thinking on this point. A man may teach his son to chip an arrowhead as a technique to be employed at once by the boy in hunting or in self-defense, as a means of preparation for adulthood, as a form of artistic expression, as a training in patience and self-control, as a step in the training of leadership, as a means of coming in contact with a divine power, or as training in a trade. The ends would, in these various instances, be utilitarian, preparatory, aesthetic, disciplinary, social, religious, or vocational. All of these objectives have existed for centuries, often simultaneously, but the emphasis has usually been only one or two at once. The main end of education in any single period of history is the one that best reflects the needs of society at the time, but less popular objectives have some followers. In short, mankind has never been able to make up its mind for long about the proper aims of education, and since there are relatively so few of them one finds the same ones cropping up in different centuries whenever the environment is appropriate for each in turn.[19]

Specific Objectives for the Christian School

What should be the educational objectives for the Christian school? The following is the statement of purpose for the Delaware County Christian School in Newtown Square, Pennsylvania.

In the Delaware County Christian School the seven cardinal goals of education, viz., character, citizenship, vocation, health, fundamental skills, worthy use of leisure, worthy home membership, are fully accepted and set forth through the curriculum. But these goals are enlarged by being integrated with an acknowledgment of the triune God and with the revelation of His truth in the Holy Scriptures. The intent is that each student shall have a knowledge of life on the broadest possible plane.

The child thus becomes spiritually fitted for a fruitful relationship to God and is brought into meaningful adjustment personally with today's complex world.[20]

Dr. Roy Lowrie, Jr., headmaster of the Delaware County Christian School for many years, lists in an article in the *Christian Teacher* twenty-two objectives for the Christian school.

1. To teach that the Lord Jesus Christ is the Son of God who came to earth to die for sin.
2. To teach the necessity of being born again through faith in the Lord Jesus Christ.
3. To teach that progress in Christian living depends upon fellowship with God through daily feeding upon the Word, prayer, and service.
4. To teach that each Christian should purpose to yield himself wholeheartedly to God, a sustained sacrifice, obeying all of His will.

5. To teach that a Christian should not, and need not, live his life under the dominion of sin.
6. To teach that the Bible is the only Word of God and is practical and important.
7. To teach that all of life must be related to God if we are to comprehend the true meaning of life.
8. To integrate academic subjects with the Bible.
9. To promote the application of biblical principles to every part of daily life.
10. To show the way a Christian should live in this present evil world.
11. To teach the urgency of world missions.
12. To teach the student to apply himself and to fulfill his responsibilities.
13. To teach the student to work independently and cooperatively.
14. To develop critical thinking.
15. To develop creative skills.
16. To develop effective skills for communication.
17. To teach the knowledge and skills required for occupational competence.
18. To teach Christian social graces.
19. To teach our American heritage and the current problems facing our country and world.
20. To develop an appreciation of the fine arts.
21. To stimulate the desire for wholesome physical and mental recreation.
22. To show the student his present civic responsibilities and to prepare him for adult citizenship with the understanding that government is ordained of God.[21]

The Wheaton Christian Grammar School catalog contains an effective presentation of well-formulated education objectives. Not only are their objectives specifically spelled out, but they are listed categorically under the headings of physical, mental, spiritual, social and emotional, all of which can be related to a Christian theistic philosophy of education. The following is a listing of their objectives under each heading:

Spiritually

"Let the Word of God dwell in you richly."
To lead the child under the guidance and power of the Holy Spirit:
to an experience of being born of the Spirit through personal faith in the Lord Jesus Christ.

into a study and personal application of the Bible so that he will
be conformed to the image of Christ Jesus.

to desire to share his spiritual experiences with others.

Mentally

"Let this mind be in you which was also in Christ Jesus."

to aid in the discovery and development of God-given intellectual abilities and to recognize the Christian obligation to
use them constructively.

to stimulate reasoning, academic investigation, creative and
critical thinking.

to impart a command of common knowledge and skills and develop ability to adapt in a rapidly changing society.

to develop the individual's mind to its maximum without losing
the ability to accept the simplicity of the Scriptures.

Physically

"Present your bodies a living sacrifice . . . unto God."

To develop:

coordination, grace, poise in movement, muscle tone and balance, endurance and agility.

worthy use of leisure time.

desirable habits in the care of the body.

a respect for the body as the temple of the Holy Spirit.

Socially

"No man liveth unto himself."

to foster respect for parents, courtesy and love for the whole
family, and to help the child assume, with understanding,
responsibility within the family unit.

to help the child show his responsibility for good sportsmanship,
honesty and concern for the rights of others by Christlike
involvement in every group to which he belongs.

to arouse and promote personal responsibility toward home and
foreign missions.

to develop an understanding, appreciation, love and respect for
all men.

Emotionally

"Be strong in the Lord and in the power of His might."
To help the child:
achieve emotional stability through a personal relationship to
the Lord Jesus Christ.
develop positive attitudes toward situations and people.
develop sensitivity to the aesthetic.
recognize the Christ-controlled personality as the source of true
happiness.[22]

This has not been an attempt to formulate a complete list of educational objectives, but only to stimulate some much-needed thinking in this area. With the basic foundational concepts clearly in mind, it is now possible to begin at least to be definitive concerning specific operationally defined educational objectives for each specific local situation. Regardless of whether it is from the viewpoint of the total school program, a specific course, or a specific class hour, there must be definite predetermined educational objectives toward which the teachers and school administration can move.

Reasons for Defining Objectives

The amazing conclusion which can be drawn when evaluating the accomplishments of a particular organization is that those having specific aims or objectives in mind can accomplish more. Even apart from this basic and fundamental reason for having objectives clearly in mind, there are several other reasons equally as important for defining the educational objectives of a Christian school.

First, a statement of our objectives clarifies the goals toward which we are aiming. Clear perspective gives direction and impetus to our daily work. We can make plans for the achievement of objectives. Such planning and its execution are right at the core of our program of Christian education. Our objectives are the targets to be hit through effective planning.

Second, a statement of our objectives gives us a standard against which we can judge the present status and the rate of progress of our school. How can we evaluate our educational program accurately if we do not have clear objectives to use for our evaluation criteria?

Third, a statement of our objectives is needed for interpreting our Christian school to the public through our public relations program. A printed statement of school objectives can be read and studied by parents who are considering the enrollment of their children in our school. These objectives help answer the question, "What is the Christian school all about?" The explanation of our objectives should be the foundation of our public relations program.[23]

Because there are essential educational objectives in the Christian school which cannot be achieved in any other kind of school, it becomes imperative, in order to maintain distinctive Christian education in the Christian school, to clearly and concisely define the objectives and the means for achieving them.

Distinctives of Christian Education Summarized

Distinctive Marks

In discussing the distinctives of Christian education and the Christian school with Dr. Roy W. Lowrie, Jr., I was introduced to the following three distinctives of Christian education:

1. A regular Bible course as a part of the curriculum.
2. Christian counseling and guidance.
3. The integration of Scripture and subject matter.[24]

These additional comments by representative leaders, engaged in Christian school work, shed more light on the distinctive marks of Christian education.

One Christian school administrator expressed that:

Christian education, in the true sense, is marked by, first of all, a sense of humility. Both teacher and student alike are sitting at the feet of the Master. This attitude eliminates the pride of intellect which is so often the hallmark of learning. Also, Christian education provides a sense of personal responsibility. Christian education provides a set of values which are not relative and changing, but which are derived from a basic point of reference, the ultimacy of God and His Word.

Another commented on the vital connection between the Christian home and the Christian school in training the child.

Christian education is basically a function of the home. Parents are commanded to "Bring up a child in the way he should go. . . ." (Deuteronomy 6, especially verses 6–7), make it clear as to the parents' obligation to educate, and that education (or training) is a full-time, 24-hours-a-day job. A Christian school supplements and complements the Christian home in the life of the child, touching every aspect of his being, training the whole child—body, soul, and spirit. This training of the "whole child" makes Christian education unique.

Distinctive Assumptions

Dr. Lowrie lists seven further distinctive basic assumptions of Christian education as well as the personal commitments of the personnel.

1. God is the Creator and sustainer of all things.
2. God maintains ultimate control over His entire universe.
3. Because of sin, man omits God from his thinking or fails to give Him His proper due.
4. Man needs to be regenerated.
5. The true meanings and values of life can be ascertained only by a regenerated person within the light of God's Person, purpose and work.
6. Commitment to the Bible as the inspired inerrant Word of God.
7. Personal commitment to the Lord Jesus Christ.[25]

Distinctive Personnel

To these assumptions should be added, first of all, a statement concerning the distinctive nature of the personnel engaged in Christian education. Though it does not necessarily follow that Christian education automatically results from personnel who are rightly related to their Creator through personal faith in Jesus Christ, it must be understood that apart from this it never can take place.

Distinctive Philosophy

The final distinctive pertains to the area of philosophy.

Why should Christians borrow a system of education from the secular world? Should we not derive from God's revelation our own philosophy, God's structure of the universe?[26] Christian education has been begging, borrowing and stealing from secular education for too long in this area.

It is understandable that an avowed opponent of Christianity like John Dewey should prefer a truthless instrumentalism; but it is a mystery how any clear thinker can consciously base his views on experience and continue to call his views Christian. The word "Christian" has a fairly definite meaning in history. It has always referred to a world view based on the Bible, and any attempt to discover Christian principles in experience as opposed to revelation empties the word of all definite meaning. If therefore a school system is to claim to be a Christian system, some guidance must be sought in revelation.[27]

With education based on a Word-centered, Christian, theistic world view and conducted by Holy Spirit-controlled Christian teachers who are attempting to integrate the whole of the pupil's personality with the truth of the Word of God and all truth, we have the ingredients necessary for obtaining the desired result of "distinctive Christian education."

PART THREE

Why Christian Education?

7

The Distinctive Purpose of God for This Age

In the words of Ayn Rand, a noted contemporary novelist, "Never before has the world been clamoring so desperately for answers to crucial problems and never before has the world been so frantically committed to the belief that no answers are possible. To reconstruct the Scripture, the modern attitude is, 'Father, forgive us, for we know not what we are doing, and please don't tell us.' "[1]

With the current intellectual winds of existentialism blowing, it seems that everything that once was nailed down is coming loose. With no emphasis on the past or the future, no belief in absolutes, and an emphasis on purposelessness for man in this life, existentialism and the philosophy of "presentism" certainly provide the philosophical framework for the "gusto generation." Almost without realizing it, many Christians have been infected with this attitude. The result has been a questioning and, in some cases, a refusal to accept concepts such as the infallibility and inerrancy of all of the Scriptures, as well as the absolute necessity of the church. In light of this, the question is appropriate: in Heaven's name, what on earth is God doing?

What is God's plan for this age? Because we believe that the first principles of any man's philosophy can never be proven but must always be accepted by faith, we start with the assumption or presupposition that the Bible in its entirety, both Old and New Testaments, is verbally inspired and without error. Building upon the foundation of God's revelation, we will answer in chapter 7 the question, "In Heaven's name, what on earth is God doing?" and in chapter 8 the question, "In Heaven's name, what on earth are we to be doing?"

What on earth is God doing? Is God's plan the *Christianization of the world* (that is, making all the world Christian)? Second Peter 3:9 is true—the Lord is ". . . not willing that any should perish, but that all should come to repentance." But the fact is that not many have or are really coming to repentance. Certainly God loved the whole world, and Christ's death was sufficient for the sins of the entire world for all time; yet the number of people who believe (*see* John 3:16) is small compared with the population explosion of 2.7 percent per year. At this rate, the world's population doubles every thirty-five years. This means that by the year 2010 the world's population will have jumped from four billion to eight billion, even though it took 1850 years of population growth to achieve the first billion.[2]

It has been estimated that 200 years ago, at the beginning of the modern-day missionary movement, Christian believers comprised 25 percent of the world's population. Today it is believed that Christianity makes up only 8 percent of the world's population. Unless there is a radical revival by the year 2000, we will be reduced to about 2 percent.[3] If God's plan is to make all the world Christian, statistics seem to indicate His plan is failing miserably. Yet, because of what we know of the character and attributes of God, we believe He cannot fail, and therefore neither will His plan. God is immutable, His character never changes, and what He has promised to do He will do. We simply must discover what His plan is.

Is God's plan the *evangelization of the world?* This relates to the heralding of the message of salvation to the ends of the earth. Mark 16:15; Matthew 28:19, 20; and Acts 1:8 are used in support of this position. A brief examination of church history shows that this plan, though not a complete failure, has not met with consistent success.

From the death of Christ, approximately A.D. 37, to the rise of Nero, A.D. 64, there occurred probably the greatest missionary thrust of all time. The missionary journeys of the Apostle Paul took the gospel to almost every corner of the known world. Though Paul himself did not go everywhere, the missionary strategy given him by the Holy Spirit led him to the key metropolitan centers of the known world. The basic pattern found in Acts 14:19–23 is a model of what he practiced everywhere he went. The result of this is a typical comment in 2 Timothy 4:17, where he states: ". . . that by me the preaching might be fully known, and that all the Gentiles [the nations] might hear."

Apparently Paul went to the church at Thessalonica, and they "became followers of us, and of the Lord, having received the word in much affliction, with joy of the Holy Ghost" (1 Thessalonians 1:6). The result is that they became "ensamples" or literally a pattern or model to all those believing in Macedonia and Achaia. Paul goes on to say, "in every place your faith to God-ward is spread abroad; so that we need not speak any thing" (v. 8).

From A.D. 64 to A.D. 313, when by Emperor Constantine's Edict of Toleration (Edict of Milan) Christianity was made the state religion, there was very little effort at world evangelization. Though Constantine's soldiers forced thousands into the sea to be baptized, there is no indication that these people really believed and therefore truly became Christians. From the fall of Rome in A.D. 476 until Martin Luther made known his Ninety-five Theses at Wittenberg in 1517, Christianity lost its evangelistic thrust.

Even though much of our great American heritage is related to the transplanting of the Protestant Reformation to this country, we do not find the modern-day missionary movement really beginning until the 1700s; and at the rate of our present population expansion, we are just not keeping pace. There really isn't anything wrong with this answer to the question, "Is God's plan the evangelization of the world?" except that in light of the Scripture, it does not go far enough and is not specifically the clear statement of Christ as to His plan.

Then what is God's plan or purpose for this age? *The building of His church.* Even though there may be some support for the first two answers, the clear statement of God's plan is given in Matthew 16:18: ". . . I will build my church; and the gates of hell shall not prevail against it." On the basis of Christ's statement, here are some preliminary observations.

1. Christ is doing the building.
2. It was yet in the future when it was to begin.
3. He is building His church ("my church").
4. Hades itself will not stop the process.
5. God's plan, though not yet begun at the time of Matthew 16:18, is designed to succeed.

Acts 15:14 says God is now calling "a people for his name," from among both the Jews and the Gentiles. But what is the church? How is it being formed? When did it begin? And what are some New Testament principles to help guide the church?

What is the church? If one checks an English concordance such as Strong's and takes the time to count the usages of the word *church,* he will discover a total of 113 references. However, using a Greek concordance such as Moulton and Geden or Smith's *Greek-English Concordance,* one discovers that there are 115 occurrences of the word *church* or *ekklesia.* Twice the word *ekklesia* is translated in the English New Testament as "assembly." There is, however, one disputed passage in Acts 2:47 which might for some reduce the total to 114. If so, then it would be 112 as "church" and twice as "assembly."

The word *ekklesia* is derived from the verb *ekkaleo,* which is a compound of the preposition *ek* or "out of" and the verb *kaleo,* which means "to call or summon."[4] Together the word now means "to call out of." Though the etymological meaning of the word itself does not support the biblical doctrine of the church as a people called out or separated from the world by God, the new term certainly does complement the rest of the New Testament teaching regarding the character and purpose of the church.

Of the 115 references to the word *ekklesia* in the New Testament, at least 85 (74 percent) of the references refer to a group of believers meeting in a specific geographical location. Approximately 15 (13 percent) of the references refer to the church, the Body of Christ, while an additional 5 of the occurrences have no reference at all to the New Testament church. Such occurrences are to be found in Acts 19:32, 41 which describe an unruly mob, while in verse 39 of the same chapter it is used again to describe a lawful assembly. The remaining ten occurrences, though they refer to the church, are difficult if not impossible to separate as to whether they refer to the local church or to the universal meaning of the church, the Body of Christ. Examples of this would be in Acts 2:47 as well as 5:11. It is not within the scope of this volume to completely discuss the church both in its technical and nontechnical usage, whether it be in the Septuagint or New Testament. So let me suggest five additional sources that will give an excellent study of the meaning and uses of the word *church,* as well as the nature of the church and its function in God's program.

1.   Radmacher, Earl D., "The Nature of the Church" doctoral dissertation, Dallas Theological Seminary, Dallas, 1962. Radmacher, Earl D., *What the Church Is All About: A Biblical and Historical Study.* Chicago: Moody Press, 1978.
2.   Saucy, Robert L., *The Church in God's Program.* Chicago: Moody Press, 1972.
3.   Hay, Alexander Rattray, *The New Testament Order for Church and Missionary.* St. Louis: New Testament Missionary Union, 1947.
4.   Richards, Lawrence O., *A New Face for the Church.* Grand Rapids: Zondervan, 1970.
5.   Stott, John R. W., *One People.* Downers Grove, Ill.: Inter-Varsity, 1968.

On the basis of the New Testament, what is the church?

The Apostle Paul in Colossians 1:18 states, "And he is the head of the body, the church: who is the beginning, the firstborn from the dead; that in all things he might have the preeminence." Again, in Ephesians 1:22, 23, Paul states, "And hath put all things under his feet, and gave him to be the head over all things to the church, Which is his body, the fulness of him that filleth all in all." The conclusion on the basis of the New Testament, and specifically the writings of the Apostle Paul, is that the church is the Body of Jesus Christ. Jesus Christ is referred to as the Head, while the church is referred to as His Body. Paul goes on to say in Ephesians 5:23 that Jesus Christ is not only the "head of the church" but He is also "the saviour of the body." Apparently, in the writings of the Apostle Paul the terms "church" and the "body of Christ" are used synonymously, and to speak of one is to specifically imply the other.

How is the church being formed? The answer to this question is made easier by the fact that if we can show how the church is being formed, then we can show how the Body of Jesus Christ is being formed. Or if the Scripture specifically gives to us the answer as to how the Body is being formed, then it is also giving to us the answer as to how the church of Jesus Christ is being formed. The Apostle Paul in 1 Corinthians 12:12, 13, as well as in Galatians 3:26–28, gives us the answer. The 1 Corinthians verses state, "For as the body is one, and hath many members, and all the members of that one body, being many, are one body: so also is Christ. For by one Spirit are we all baptized [identified] into one body, whether we be Jews or Gentiles, whether we be bond or free; and have been all made to drink into one Spirit." The Galatians reference states, "For ye are all the children of God by faith in Christ Jesus. For as many of you as have been baptized [identified] into Christ have put on Christ. There is neither Jew nor Greek, there is neither bond nor free, there is neither male nor female: for ye are all one in Christ Jesus."

On the basis of Paul's statement in 1 Corinthians 12, it is the baptism of the Holy Spirit that is placing all believers, whether they be Jew or Gentile, into the one body, which we

can assume on the basis of his other writings to the Body of
Christ or the church. However, Paul does not stop with simply
the matter of identifying believers with one another as part of
the Body of Christ, but in Galatians 3 he goes one step further
and shows that the baptism of the Holy Spirit is the identifying
or placing of the believer into the Person of Jesus Christ Himself. Not only have we been identified in the larger grouping
called the church or the Body of Christ, but each believer has
been individually wrapped around or enveloped into the Person
of Jesus Christ.

The beauty of this picture is that God is not only dealing
with us as a large group but uniquely, as individuals, as well. As
a part of the Body of Christ, God is not only concerned with us
as His people, but is concerned with us as persons, and so places
each one of us into Himself through the ministry of the Holy
Spirit in baptism. On the basis of the two passages of Scripture
that we have considered, a definition of the baptism of the Holy
Spirit would be: "the placing or the identification of the believer into the Body of Christ (1 Corinthians 12:12, 13), which is
the church (Colossians 1:18 and Ephesians 1:22, 23), as well as
the placing of the believer into the Person of Jesus Christ Himself (Galatians 3:26–28)." How is the church being formed? The
church of Jesus Christ, which is the Body of Christ, is being
formed in this age by means of the baptism of the Holy Spirit.

When did the church begin? The first occurrence of the
word *church* or *ekklesia* is found in Matthew 16:18. These are
the words of Jesus Christ Himself when He said, "I will build
my church." The interesting thing is that there are only three
references in Matthew to the word *church*, and these are found
once in Matthew 16:18 and twice in Matthew 17. These are the
only references to the word *church* in all of the Gospels. As
Saucy points out, it is also absent from 2 Timothy, Titus, 1
Peter, 2 Peter, 1 John, 2 John, and Jude.[5]

But when did the church begin? Apparently it was still in
the future when Jesus spoke of it in Matthew 16:18. So where do
we go to place the beginning of the New Testament church?
Normally Acts 2 is used to mark the beginning of the New Tes-

tament church, the Body of Christ. But how can one prove that
the church began in Acts 2? Again, our task has been made easier because we have been able to understand that the church is
the Body of Christ and that the church and/or the Body is being
formed by the ministry of the Holy Spirit in baptism. Thus, if
we can show where the church first began, we can also show
where the Body of Christ actually was first formed. Also, if we
can show when the baptism of the Holy Spirit first took place,
we will be able to show where the church began. Using the
baptism of the Holy Spirit, I believe we will be able to show not
only where it first took place, but also then where the church—
the Body of Christ—actually began.

   To begin with, the baptism of the Holy Spirit is conspicu-
ous by its absence in the Old Testament. Never is this concept
to be found in all of the thirty-nine books of the Old Testament.
Even Dr. Leon Wood in his book, *The Holy Spirit in the Old
Testament,* agrees that beyond a shadow of a doubt, the one
ministry of the Holy Spirit that is not to be found in the Old
Testament is Holy Spirit baptism.[6] When one moves to the New
Testament one discovers that the baptism of the Holy Spirit is
referred to by Jesus Christ Himself in all of the Gospels as well
as in the book of Acts. In each case it is always referred to as
something that is yet future. Matthew 3:11, Mark 1:8, Luke
3:16, John 1:26–28, 31–34 all refer to the fact that "John indeed
baptized with water, but ye shall be baptized $ἐν$ [into the sphere
of or by means of] the Holy Spirit." In each case, the reference
to the baptism is clearly future.

   When we come to the book of Acts (1:5), again our Lord
makes reference to the baptism of the Holy Spirit when He says,
"For John truly baptized with water; but ye shall be baptized
with [or by means of] the Holy Spirit not many days hence."
Apparently now the reference that our Lord makes to the baptism of the Holy Spirit, even though it is still in the future, is
clearly a reference to something that is about to take place in
just a few short days.

   The problem now is, how do we know for sure that the
baptism of the Holy Spirit took place for the first time on the

Day of Pentecost? Even though there are a number of references in Acts 2 to an unusual outpouring of the ministry of the Holy Spirit on the believers who were gathered together on the Day of Pentecost, one must conclude that there is no clear statement in Acts 2 that the baptism of the Holy Spirit in fact actually did occur. This at first might seem to be confusing, but apparently even the believers gathered together on the Day of Pentecost did not fully understand that which took place. Some of the phenomena of that particular day they were to clearly discern and understand, but the ministry of the Holy Spirit in baptism as a nonexperiential outpouring of the Holy Spirit was something that was not discernible at that point in their spiritual understanding. It is not until we go to Acts 10 and 11 that we have spelled out for us the answer that we thought we would find in Acts 2.

In Acts 10, we have the account of Peter's vision on the rooftop and our Lord's command to go to the Gentiles, even though Peter considered them to be unclean. In the vision, our Lord made it very clear to Peter that he was not to call something unclean that the Lord was calling clean. While Peter was trying to figure out the meaning of the vision, a man appeared at the door, having been sent from Cornelius, and called and asked if Simon Peter were lodging there. Peter pondered the vision, and the Spirit said unto him, ". . . Behold, three men seek thee. Arise therefore, and get thee down, and go with them, doubting nothing: for I have sent them." Peter then went to Cornelius's house, and in 10:44–48 we have the description of what took place while Peter was proclaiming (preaching) unto them the Lord Jesus. Right in the middle of Peter's sermon, the Holy Spirit fell on them which heard the Word of God and the believing Jews who were with him were astonished because the gift of the Holy Spirit was poured out on the Gentiles. They began to speak with tongues and magnify God and Peter said, "Can any man forbid water, that these should not be baptized, which have received the Holy Ghost as well as we?"

All of this raised a furor among the leaders of the Jerusalem church. A council was called, and the "Jerusalem Ministerial

Association" demanded that Peter give an explanation of what had taken place in the house of this Gentile, Cornelius. I am sure that if Peter had not been able to give a satisfactory answer to these Jewish leaders at the church of Jerusalem, he certainly would have been defrocked and excommunicated from the "Jerusalem Ministerial Council." However, Acts 11:4 says, "But Peter rehearsed the matter from the beginning, and expounded it by order unto them saying." Literally what the Scripture is saying to us is that Peter began at the beginning and explained to them in logical and chronological order, step by step, exactly every detail of what had taken place, both prior to his going to the house of Cornelius, as well as the specific events that occurred as he began to preach. The heart of his explanation is found in 11:15–17: "And as I began to speak, the Holy Ghost fell on them, as on us at the beginning. Then remembered I the word of the Lord, how that he said, John indeed baptized with water; but ye shall be baptized with the Holy Ghost. Forasmuch then as God gave them the like gift as he did unto us, who believed on the Lord Jesus Christ; what was I, that I could withstand God?" What was the response to this? "When they heard these things, they held their peace, and glorified God, saying, Then hath God also to the Gentiles granted repentance unto life" (v. 8).

This is what Peter told the Jerusalem council: "While I was speaking, the Holy Spirit fell on the Gentiles at Cornelius's house as He had on us—that is, the Jews at the beginning." What is this *beginning* that Peter is referring to? We can narrow it down between Acts 1:5 and 10:44. Because we have been able to narrow it down this much, the task of determining the beginning has been greatly simplified. One simply has to discern where did this event take place for the first time? The only conclusion available is what happened to the Jews on the Day of Pentecost.

Peter goes on to say, "I put two and two together when I remembered the Word of the Lord—'John indeed baptized with water, but ye shall be baptized with [or by means of] the Holy Spirit.' " Peter concludes his testimony by saying that apparently God had given to the Gentiles the same gift that He had given to the Jews, and who in the world was he to withstand God. Peter's testimony was so clear and penetratingly convincing that the leaders of the church at Jerusalem stopped interrogating Peter and began praising the Lord.

When did the baptism of the Holy Spirit take place for the first time? Apparently on the basis of the testimony of the Apostle Peter in Acts 11:15–17, the baptism of the Holy Spirit took place for the first time on the Day of Pentecost.

We have been able to discern, from the Scriptures, God's plan for this age in relationship to the church. First, the church is the Body of Christ, and it is being formed by the ministry of the Holy Spirit in baptism. We have been able to discern from Scripture that even though the first reference to the word *church* in the New Testament is found in Matthew 16:18, the church, the Body of Christ, does not actually begin until Acts 2. By showing that the baptism of the Holy Spirit first took place with the Jews that were gathered together at the beginning (the Day of Pentecost), we are able to conclude that the baptism of the Holy Spirit, which is the means whereby God is forming the church, the Body of Christ, did in fact take place for the first time on the Day of Pentecost.

The tragedy is that even though the world of the first century and the world of the twentieth century are civilizations in comparison, having many similarities, it appears that the church of the first century and the church of the twentieth century stand in contrast. Even though everyone is desirous of having a New Testament church, in far too many cases churches are governed by norms acquired from tradition rather than the New Testament. Because we have followed traditional norms rather than New Testament norms, the church today is confused. Though very much alive, it seems to be sick when compared with the New Testament.

What are some norms from the New Testament that will help to guide us in the establishment of churches that are uniquely and distinctively New Testament?

(1) Local churches consist of Christians, not buildings. The

truth of the New Testament is that God no longer dwells in buildings, but He dwells in the bodies of all of His children (Galatians 2:20; 1 Corinthians 6:19). Every born-again believer has the indwelling presence not only of the Holy Spirit, but also of Jesus Christ Himself. However, it is true that because of our own cultural situation, the use of buildings facilitates the ministry of the local church. The important emphasis should not be placed upon buildings, but on the believers who are meeting together. Christians today need to understand that the building itself is not the church, but that the believers who gather together and meet in that specific geographical location are in fact the church, the Body of Christ. Verses of Scripture that one might study in order to focus on this truth are Acts 16:4, 5; 2 Corinthians 11:28; 1 Corinthians 4:17, 7:17, 11:18; Romans 16:3, 4, 16.

(2) Local churches are to meet on the first day of the week. Eight times throughout the New Testament, reference is made to meeting on the first day of the week.[7] This apparently was in observance of the fact that the Lord Jesus Christ Himself arose from the grave not on the Sabbath, Saturday, but on Sunday, the first day of the week. The fact that they met on the first day of the week does not indicate that they did not meet on other days. Nor does it limit our meetings only to the first day of the week. Thirteen times, six in the book of Acts, reference is made to doing something daily. As Francis Schaeffer says, our meeting together on the first day of the week is a testimony to the fact that "He is risen, He is risen indeed."[8] Believing that the Bible provides principles that are supra- or transcultural, and believing that this is a principle that has been established for us in the New Testament regardless of what other days or what other times believers may meet together, the New Testament assumes that believers will be meeting together regularly on the first day of the week (1 Corinthians 16:2; Acts 20:7).

(3) There are to be church officers. The New Testament church had its leadership, and these leaders consisted primarily of elders and deacons. True, the New Testament uses the terms "elder" and "bishop" synonymously, but the interesting fact is that never is the term "elder" used in the singular in relation-

ship to a specific church.[9] Apparently each of the New Testament churches had a plurality of elders. While we would agree that the pastor is to be one of those elders, the New Testament is conveying to us that there be more than one elder for the church in each geographical location.

The question that arises then is whether or not the elders are only the ordained ministerial staff—in other words, the paid, professional staff for each church—or whether there can be lay elders in a given congregation. Apparently the New Testament does not conclusively answer this question for us, although there is serious question that can be raised regarding the eligibility of a young man, fresh out of a Bible school or seminary, as being one who qualifies biblically for the role of elder. Apparently the wisdom of age was something that was assumed when the New Testament spoke of an elder. Though the specific age is not given, maturity and the years of life-experience were considered far more than the fact that the individual had a diploma or a degree. Whether the elders in a given local church are the ordained, paid, professional staff or whether lay elders are also considered, the norm of the New Testament requires a plurality of leadership.

I am also aware of the fact that the elders were the decision-making body in the New Testament church, while the deacons, though not directly involved in decision-making, were the ones to serve and minister to the needs of the church. It seems that in many of our churches today the deacons, or at least a portion of them, are actually functioning as elders. I believe this should be recognized. A plurality of elders apparently was to insure the balance of all of the decisions that were made, preventing any one individual from becoming a "dictator" for a local church. Although the New Testament church started immediately with elders, it was not until a need arose regarding serving tables and ministering to the needs of the widows that the deacons were selected (Acts 6; cf. Acts 20:17–38 and 1 Timothy 5:17).

(4) There are specific qualifications for elders and deacons. For an excellent, thorough study of these qualifications one

needs to use the study guide provided by Dr. Gene Getz in his book *The Measure of a Man* (Regal Press). The crucial question is whether or not all these qualities must be found in the individuals who are going to be serving and ministering in the church. If a man did not measure up to these qualities in every area, apparently, on the basis of the New Testament, even though he truly was gifted (Ephesians 4:7), he was unfit for the office of elder or deacon. Basically, the lists of qualities or qualifications as given in 1 Timothy 3:1–7, 8–13; Titus 1:5–9; and Acts 6:1–6 are the same for both elder and deacon.

The one addition specifically for elders is that they be "apt to teach." It is not clear from the Timothy passage whether the individual to be selected as an elder had to have taught, or actually be teaching. In fact, it is possible to accurately translate 1 Timothy 3:2 as "teachable" rather than implying the gift of the ability to teach. Probably both of these ideas are at least somewhat involved. In order for one to be a teacher or a leader, he first must have a teachable spirit. It is not necessary to require that specific teaching experience is assumed in the phrase "apt to teach" in 1 Timothy 3.

(5) The New Testament church must take discipline seriously. I recall a professor in seminary who would say, "Show me a church that believes in and practices New Testament church discipline, and I'll show you a New Testament church." Church discipline alone is not the criterion for determining whether or not a church is in fact true to the New Testament, but the church that is endeavoring to be a New Testament church will take seriously the teaching that the New Testament clearly gives regarding discipline.

First Corinthians 5:1–5 is an example of this and one that we cannot pass off easily. Apparently public sins should be dealt with publicly, while private sins are to be dealt with privately. Because there are some things that take place publicly, they not only affect the individual or individuals involved, but they also reflect on the ministry of the church, the Body of Christ. If an individual is involved in this kind of public sin, then the ministry of the Gospel is in fact going to be hindered if the individual is not willing to care for the matter. The New Testament is clearly teaching that it is the right and the responsibility of the local church to administer church discipline.

This is not an attempt to destroy the individual or to make a public spectacle of him or of the sin that has been committed, but is an attempt to allow Satan to sift the individual and thereby have the individual restored, not only to fellowship personally with the Lord Himself, but with the local church (1 Corinthians 5).

(6) There is to be fellowship between local congregations of believers. We have already touched on Acts 11 and the Jerusalem council (also Acts 15) and have discerned the fact that when difficult questions arose in the early church, they were not resolved by one individual or specific church, but by all of the churches meeting together, discerning the mind of Christ. Not only is there a need for church fellowship in regard to the resolving of internal and practical issues, but there is also the need of believers from local churches fellowshipping together to encourage one another in their growth in grace and the knowledge of the Lord.

(7) The Lord's supper and baptism are the two ordinances of the New Testament that are to be practiced. Baptism in the New Testament may include the following: (a) The use of the preposition $\acute{\epsilon}\nu$ refers to the means or instrument (instrumentality) of our baptism—as in, baptized by means of the Holy Spirit (Acts 1:5). (b) The use of the preposition $\acute{\epsilon}\iota s$ refers to the sphere with, or into which, we have been identified. It has reference to Holy Spirit baptism and also has the visible means of water baptism in view (Matthew 28:19—primary, water; secondary, Holy Spirit: Romans 6:3—primary, Holy Spirit; secondary, water).

Matthew 28:19, 20 (water, Holy Spirit), Acts 2:41 (water), Acts 8:36–39 (water), as well as 1 Corinthians 11:20–34 (Lord's table) are passages that clearly teach that the Lord's supper and baptism are to be practiced by New Testament believers as they meet together as part of the church, the Body of Christ. The Lord's supper was not only for believers to reflect back on the death of Christ on their behalf, but also to look forward to the coming of Christ again for His church. There is also the inward look as believers are exhorted to examine themselves, lest they eat and drink in an "unworthy manner."

Baptism was also practiced by the New Testament church. The necessity of baptism for membership in a local congregation today is a much disputed point. The argument goes that if there is no "right" that makes one a member of the Body of Christ, then there ought not to be a specific "right" to allow one the privilege to join a local church. Baptism was, however, the outward testimony both to the believers as well as to the unsaved regarding the spiritual transformation that had taken place in the life of the individual believer. That baptism was the practice of the New Testament church is evident from the record of Acts. "They that gladly received his word were baptized . . ." (Acts 2:41). And in Acts 8:36, the Ethiopian eunuch asked, "What doth hinder me to be baptized?" Even the previous references that we have made to Peter and Cornelius's house show they were baptized immediately after their conversion. F. F. Bruce concludes that "the idea of an unbaptized Christian is simply not entertained in the New Testament."[10]

Three additional New Testament guidelines must also be given consideration. (1) The primary function of the church meeting is to minister to the spiritual needs of Christian believers, not non-Christians. Acts 2:42–44 gives us a picture of what transpired as the believers gathered together for their meetings. The only reference in the New Testament to the unsaved being in the congregation with the believers as they met together is in 1 Corinthians 14:23, 24. This obviously is in the context of speaking in tongues. Paul says, "if they are there," and the Greek construction is a third-class conditional clause which conveys the idea of probability. Probably they won't be there, but if they are it would be better for them to hear you prophesying, to proclaim the Word, than to hear you speaking in tongues. Prophecy they could understand, while speaking in tongues would cause them to think you were crazy. We will examine this New Testament norm further in chapter 8 as we examine God's program for this age.

(2) Evangelism should be done by the church as a whole rather than by the pastor alone. According to Ephesians 4, the responsibility of the pastor-teacher is to "equip the saints unto the work of ministering." The result is that the believers or the Body of Christ not only are ministering to "one another," but ministering to the needs of the lost world. Only then can the Body be built up and edified.

Obviously just the practicality of the situation helps us to understand that a lost world cannot be reached by one man or even a handful of men, even if all of the pastors would be engaged in the ministry of evangelism. I realize Vance Havner's statement is not actually a biblical statement, but I believe it will help us focus on the situation when he reminds us of the responsibility that the pastor and the people have in relationship to evangelism. He asks the question, "Who gives birth to the baby lambs, the shepherd or the sheep?" Though the Apostle Paul clearly exhorts young Timothy to "do the work of an evangelist," the writings of Paul and the other New Testament writers clearly delineate that the role and responsibility of the pastor is to be the teacher, to feed the flock, to equip the saints, so that believers can function in *their* responsibility to take the message of the gospel to the lost where they are.

The fact that the New Testament norm indicates that the unsaved are not going to be primarily in the church further necessitates the believer taking the message of the gospel to the lost where they are. There is not one single solitary command in all of the New Testament to bring the lost to church in order to find the Savior. There are, however, multiplied commandments in the New Testament for the believer to take the message of the gospel to the lost where they are.

(3) The time, number of services, and length of services are not the crucial issues. I heard once of the church that changed the time of their services on Sunday morning so that their morning service was ending at 11:00 A.M. rather than beginning at that time. One dear lady in the church became greatly concerned about this because she felt that as they were all going home from church at eleven o'clock, God was just coming. Though the New Testament church met on the first day of the

week, whether they met at 9:00, 9:30 or 9:45, and whether or not they had Sunday school and worship back-to-back, or whether or not they came at 6:00, 7:00 or 7:30, or whether they had one or two services in the evening, were never issues raised in the New Testament. Apparently the New Testament is giving to us the freedom and flexibility to be able to structure our services in terms of number as well as time and length in order to best meet the needs of our particular flock.

In addition to these guidelines or norms from the New Testament, we must constantly remind ourselves that the crucial issue in relationship to the church is not growth in numbers and finances, but the question of whether or not we are scriptural. Do we follow the New Testament principles, and do we measure up to the established norms of the New Testament that we are aware of? If what we are doing does measure up to the established New Testament norms, regardless of whether or not it measures up to the traditional patterns or traditional forms, then we are a New Testament church and what we are doing will meet the needs of the believers and unbelievers.

This principle is true—you can only move as fast as you can educate. Today the crucial issue is whether or not we can educate people regarding the biblical answers to such questions as, What is the church? How is the church being formed? When did it begin? And what are the New Testament principles and norms that govern the functioning of the church?

8

The Distinctive Program of God for This Age

In Heaven's name, what on earth are we to be doing? Some time ago, while speaking at a Christian-school rally, a visiting pastor came to me after the service and announced, "We've thrown out worship in our church; we've left all that junk to the liberals. The most important thing in our church is that we really study the Bible." A few years ago a keynote speaker at a Sunday-school conference was sharing with pastors that over ninety people had come forward at the close of the previous Sunday-morning service. When asked how many were actually first-time decisions, he readily admitted that the percentage was small. The most perceptive question, however, was asked next when a dear pastor said, "Sir, of the first-time decisions, how many would you be able to account for one year from now?" With a slight shrug of the shoulders and a smile on his face the speaker responded, "If we're lucky, one out of four; but what difference does it make? The only issue is to preach the gospel and see that souls are saved."

What on earth are we to be doing? On the one hand, the church is saying, "The most important emphasis is Bible study," while on the other hand the church is saying, "The most important emphasis is evangelism, soul winning." As if this were not enough confusion, a third movement has risen on the horizon with the emphasis on fellowship. To this group, the most important thing is to meet together and share in the *koinonia*, the fellowship that believers experience as a part of the Body of Christ.

Well, what is it? Is it Bible study? Second Timothy 2:15 is very clear that the believer is to "study [be eager] to shew thyself approved unto God, a workman that needeth not to be ashamed, rightly dividing the word of truth." Personal and corporate Bible study are important and cannot be underestimated.

What about worship? We will look more extensively at this subject later in this chapter; however, it is sufficient at this point simply to state that John 4:23 is still in the Bible: ". . . for the Father seeketh such to worship him." In other words, an individual believer or believers corporately as a part of the church have no prerogative to decide to throw out worship. God the Father is seeking it, and it behooves us as believers to practice it.

What about fellowship? Acts 2:42–44 gives to us a pattern of what was done when the believers met together in the New Testament church. The passage specifically says that they not only "continued stedfastly in the apostles' doctrine," but also in "fellowship."

In Heaven's name, what on earth is the church to be doing? When all else fails, follow the instructions. The Bible, verbally inspired and inerrant in its entirety, gives to us not what God would say if He were here, but what God is saying because He is here. The Bible has a more relevant answer to the apparent dilemma that we face than even tomorrow morning's newspaper. The Great Commission repeated for us in all of the Gospels and in Acts does not need to be reissued. It needs only to be properly understood and then properly implemented.

The first passage we will examine is Matthew 28:16-20. Usually when one goes to the Great Commission of Matthew 28, he examines only verses 19 and 20. Believing that we must get the entire thought of this commission, we will go back to the paragraph division which begins at verse 16. "Then the eleven disciples went to Galilee, into a mountain where Jesus had appointed them." There is first the response of obedience on the part of the eleven disciples to go to the place where Jesus had told them to meet Him. Verse 17 now provides for us, I believe, the key that to a great extent unlocks the truth of the Great Commission of Matthew 28. "And when they saw him, they worshipped him: but some doubted." When the disciples saw the resurrected Lord, their personal response toward Him was one of worship. True, verse 17 says that some doubted, but not in the sense that these disciples totally disbelieved. It was more of an issue of having questions that were unresolved or unanswered. Certainly a key question that must have been in their minds, as it had been in the mind of every Jewish leader from Daniel's day to the ascension of Christ, was the question of the restoration of the kingdom. In spite of the fact that there was some doubt regarding unanswered questions, there apparently was the personal response of worship on the part of the eleven disciples toward their resurrected Lord.

But why is worship so important, and why should every child of God be a worshiper? The study of the Word demands a personal response. There's no such thing as neutrality, either positively in relation to salvation or negatively in rejecting God's plan. The Word clearly demands a response. John 1:11, 12 says that Jesus Christ "came unto his own [creation], and His own [people] received him not. But as many as received him [personally responded], to them gave he power [right or authority] to become the sons of God, even to them that believe [personally respond] on his name." The striking negative contrast to this is found in Romans 1:21 which states, "When they knew God, they glorified him not as God. . . ."

Another important consideration is that we have been created as beings who respond to love. Psychologist Diana

Baumrind of the University of California at Berkeley studied three groups of nursery-school children to determine "the best way to raise a child so he'll be both happy and competent." The parents of one of the groups under study were permissive, undemanding, insecure about how to influence their children, not at all organized in running their households, somewhat warm toward the kids but tending to baby them. A second group of parents were authoritative. They ran better-coordinated households, set clear rules and gave reasons, demanded much, but were consistent, loving, and secure in handling their children, and trained them in independence. The third group were authoritarian. They gave no reasons for their directives, except perhaps "an absolute moral imperative," and they did not encourage kids to express themselves when the children disagreed with their parents.

You guessed it. The parents who followed the middle course were the most successful. The children of the authoritarian parents, says the researcher, were "less content, more insecure and apprehensive . . . more likely to become hostile . . . under stress." Children with permissive parents were dependent and immature. The most competent and mature of all were the children of authoritative parents—that is, parents who were firm and demanding, but loving and understanding. Their children were self-reliant, self-controlled, realistic, well-adjusted to others, eager to explore.[1]

Thus, as God created life, He created beings who demand love, and this love demands a personal response.

Another reason for worship is the element of fellowship in the Christian life, which also demands a personal response. The invitation in Revelation 3:20 is, "Behold, I stand at the door, and knock: if any man hear my voice, and open the door, I will come in to him, and will sup with him, and he with me." Although this invitation may be applicable in principle to the initial salvation or conversion experience, the context of this verse (chapters 2 and 3) clearly indicates the church and relates to born-again believers. Thus the picture of verse 20 is that of Jesus Christ standing at the believer's door, individually or corporately as the church, and asking to come in. The result of the positive response of opening the door will be tremendous personal, intimate fellowship.

Certainly all these reasons for worship seem valid. But as the pastor who wanted to throw out worship listened, he still wasn't convinced. "What I need," he went on, "is a direct statement from the Word that God really puts a priority on worship either equal to, or more than, Bible study."

I responded by explaining that worship is not a prerequisite to Bible study, and so is not more important. However, worship is important because it is in relation to worship that the concept of "seeking God" is seen in the Scriptures. In Genesis 3, after Adam and Eve had eaten of the "forbidden fruit," it was God the Father who came seeking for their fellowship in the cool of the evening. The Apostle Paul says there are ". . . none that seeketh after God" (Romans 3:11), but Luke records the fact that "the Son of man is come to seek and to save that which was lost" (Luke 19:10). It is Jesus Christ who is seeking to save lost mankind. The aspect of seeking God usually left out is found in John 4:23: ". . . for the Father is seeking for those who would be continually [present tense in the Greek] worshiping Him." It's true that we're not commanded to worship, and we are commanded to study the Word (2 Timothy 2:15). Bible study is important because of what we get out of it, while worship is important because of what God gets out of it. Why God wants my expression of love is beyond my comprehension, but the biblical fact remains—God is seeking my continual worship.

The chairman of the board of American Telephone and Telegraph once said, "People are always down on what they're not up on." My pastor friend was no exception. Because of a misconception of what worship really is (an external emotional experience involving "religious idols"), he was convinced it was "out" for believers in the evangelical church.

Some years ago Mr. D. K. Reisinger, then president of the Evangelical Teacher Training Association, called many pastors all over the country and asked them to define worship without the aid of books and notes. To his amazement, not one pastor called was able to define worship adequately. Describe it, yes; but to define it satisfactorily, no.

The word *worship* comes from an old English word *worthship*, which conveys the idea of extolling the worthiness of God. The Greek word for worship is prefixed by the preposition *pros* (προς), which conveys the idea of a face-to-face meeting or relationship. *Worship* means considering or contemplating the worthiness of God through the experience of person-to-person fellowship. In worship, the Christian adores and fellowships with God personally. This then is the believer's expression of love to God.

In John 4:26, Jesus Christ replied to the Samaritan woman's statement about the Messiah by saying, "I that speak unto thee am he." As soon as the woman recognized who He was and apparently responded and was truly transformed, she was no longer concerned with the question, where do we worship? Jesus Christ had clearly shown her that the issue was *who* do you worship and how. As the woman at the well recognized the worthiness of the person with whom she was conversing, she began to respond in worship. The definition of *worship* is: "My personal response to my recognition of God as seen primarily in the Word of God." True worship involves an active personal response on the part of a person who has trusted Christ and has seen God reveal Himself in His Word.

According to the Bible, worship is not a prerequisite for Bible study, but rather the converse would be true. We read in passages such as Isaiah 6, Matthew 28:16–20 and John 4 that the Word of God properly understood causes a response of worship of God. Bible study as an end in itself will produce spiritual stagnation. To study the Word and see God reveal Himself and then respond in worship will produce spiritual stimulation or motivation for service. We are saved to serve, not sit, soak and sour; for the motivating or propelling force for service comes as a result of worship.

Christ said in John 4:24, "God is a Spirit, and he must be worshiped in the sphere of, or by means of, the Holy Spirit." One cannot worship God in one's own strength, just as nothing in the Christian life can be accomplished apart from the filling or control of the Holy Spirit. Whether it's witnessing (Acts 1:8), praying (Romans 8:26), Bible study (1 Corinthians 2:14, 15), worshiping (John 4:24), or just the step-by-step walk of the Christian life (Galatians 5:16), these are impossible unless the believer is rightly related to the Holy Spirit and thus spiritually empowered (Ephesians 5:18; Galatians 5:16).

The phrase, "in truth," is usually described by commentators as coming to the Lord in an attitude of truthfulness or honesty. This simply means you're not playing the game of worshiping just on the outside, but that your heart is right and you honestly desire to worship God on the inside. This certainly is involved. However, there is only one preposition, *in*, for both the words *Spirit* and *truth*. If you are going to translate the verse as "by means of," it must be "by means of Spirit and truth." We conclude then that the believer worships God the Father by means of the Holy Spirit and by means of the Truth, Jesus Christ (John 14:6). Thus, in worship the Trinity is brought into focus in perfect harmony and balance. I am able to respond to God the Father in worship because of my relationship to His Son, Jesus Christ, and the blessed Holy Spirit. Because of this relationship I am able to respond in an attitude of true love, praise and adoration of Him for who He is, and also to Him for what He has done to me and for me.

To review:

Why worship? Because God the Father is seeking for those who would be continually worshiping Him (John 4:23).

What is worship? It is my personal response to my recognition of God as seen primarily in the Word of God. It is the child of God looking into the face of God the Father and saying, "Father, I love You." True worship involves an active personal response on the part of a person who has trusted Christ and has seen God reveal Himself in His Word. Apparently worship is not a prerequisite for Bible study, but true worship comes as a result of study or knowledge of the Person and work of God the Father. The Word of God properly studied will prepare us for the worship of God, which should result in our being willing workers for God.

How do we worship? Although it's possible to worship God

on the outside and never worship on the inside, the converse is not true. If one is really centering his thoughts and attitude (heart) on God, this will be done outwardly through an expression of praise and adoration. Remember, the Samaritan woman made an issue of where we worship, while Christ raised the issue of who and how to worship. True worship must be of God the Father by means of a personal relationship with His Son, Jesus Christ (the Truth), and energized or empowered by means of the Holy Spirit. Because of this relationship, I am able to respond in an attitude of true love, praise, and adoration of Him for who He is, and also to Him for what He has done to me and for me.

Let's make it clear: there is no worship without knowledge. Therefore, it must be understood that not only is instruction in the basic principles of worship crucial, but so is the teaching of the Word. You will only know as much of God as you know of His Son, Jesus Christ, and you will only know as much of Jesus Christ as you know of the Word. Therefore, to respond meaningfully in worship to God is dependent upon and initiated by instruction in the Word.

Next, we should understand the basic elements of worship.

1. *Bible study.* It's true that if the passage or the truth is a familiar one, it would not have to be studied. But we must remember that the mere reading of the Word without understanding is not sufficient preparation. In some cases, Bible study may come at an earlier time, but keep in mind that worship is dependent upon knowledge. Bible study through which God the Father speaks to us personally is preparation for worship.

2. *Prayer.* This is not the meaningless repetition of words, but speaking to God out of the innermost recesses of the heart. This is also an essential part of preparation for worship, both personal and group.

3. *Music.* We know that atmosphere plays an important part in producing a real and vitalizing expression of worship. Music has a key role in producing a satisfying and orderly program. In general, we think of the organ or piano as necessary instruments because they have always been available, but the

guitar, ukulele, and even the harmonica are being successfully used—with discretion. Group singing and well-chosen special numbers are appropriate.

4. *Offering.* This is a part of our stewardship and should also be considered an expression of worship. Here we dedicate not only our money, but whole self, time, and talent to the Lord.

In addition to these four "building blocks" of worship, effective use may be made of stories, visuals, poetry, and testimonies. The use of carefully planned (not canned) testimony times along with group singing can in many cases be the capstone to a meaningful worship time.

Here are some further principles to consider in planning worship time:

1. Worship should grow out of the desire of the group and should meet their needs.
2. It should have one central theme or aim.
3. It should be geared to the needs of the group.
4. It should be planned and presented by the group.
5. It should move without disruption.
   Quiet music can be used to tie things together meaningfully, as well as to fill potential dead spots. Any announcement should be given preferably before or after the worship program or at least should not break the trend of thought.
6. It should be built upon a knowledge of the Person of God as seen in His Word. Bible study (or knowledge) is a prerequisite.
7. It should begin on schedule and end promptly.

The fact that you know the principles and even have had a brief worship service doesn't mean you or anyone else really worshiped. Answer the following questions to analyze your worship experience.

1. What was your attitude when you came into the room?
2. What was the purpose or theme of this worship time?
3. Did your attitude change as the service progressed?

4. From your experience, would you say you worshiped?
5. Did God speak to you?
6. Did you speak to God?
7. What did you feel?
8. What idea was impressed on your mind and heart?
9. As a result of this worship experience what, if anything, will you be influenced to do?
10. If you failed to experience meaningful worship, do you know why?

If you are still having problems experiencing meaningful worship, perhaps it would be helpful to review the basics of "what is worship?" and "how to worship." By applying the biblical and practical guidelines, worship should become a meaningful expression of your love relationship to the Lord. Remember, "God the Father is seeking for those who would be continually worshiping Him" (John 4:23).

The amazing conclusion that one can draw from the study of worship in the Scripture is that wherever you find one who is a worshiper, you always find one who is a willing worker. Whether the occasion is Isaiah 6, John 4, or Matthew 28, the moment that the individual or individuals involved meaningfully express their love or worship to God, they find themselves sufficiently motivated to come down out of the grandstands and get involved on the playing field. This is what happened to the eleven disciples as a result of their response of worship to the Lord in Matthew 28:18. "And Jesus approaching toward them, face to face, talked with them saying, 'To me was given all authority in heaven and on the earth.'" Apparently Matthew is reemphasizing in verse 18 the fact that there was this personal face-to-face contact or relationship between our Lord and the eleven disciples. Recognizing the doubt, the unanswered questions that they had, He responded to His disciples by telling them that not only had all authority in Heaven and earth been given to Him, but He in turn was giving it to them in preparation for His sending them out.

Now, verse 17: "Going [or "in your going" or "having

gone"] therefore, make disciples [or disciple all the nations], baptizing them into the name of the Father, and of the Son, and of the Holy Spirit." Actually, there are four verbs in verses 19, 20: *go, teach* (or really, *make disciples*), *baptizing,* and *teaching.* However, the main verb is the only one that is in the imperative form. That is the word translated "teach" or literally, "make disciples." In other words, the only verb that is actually found in the command or the imperative form all the way from verse 16 to the end of the chapter is the one verb, "teach" or "disciple."[2]

What then happened to the command "go" in the Great Commission of Matthew 28:19? Actually, there has not been a command to go as such, except possibly as a weak command. The only explanation for translating the participle of Matthew 28:19 as the command to "go" is the fact that a participle is the weakest verb form in the language and as such can assume the qualities or characteristics of the verb that follows it. In this case, it is a verb in the command or the imperative form. If it is to be translated as a command, it almost must be spoken in order to show the difference between the thrust of these two commands: "Go *MAKE DISCIPLES!"* The result of the worship experience that the disciples had sufficiently motivated them to become involved in service for their Lord. The question for them was not, "Lord, do we have to go?" but, "Lord, what do you want us to do?" Thus Jesus responded in verse 19 by saying "going," or "in your going," or "having gone, therefore, disciple the nations." The going was assumed as a result of the worship of our Lord by the disciples. The expression of love or worship sufficiently motivated them to come down out of the grandstands and get involved on the playing field. The only thing our Lord had to do was to clarify for them what they should do.

This leads us to the next question. What does it mean to make disciples? Some believe that making disciples is simply winning souls, making converts, while others seem to believe that making disciples is involved with the emphasis on teaching and helping people to grow in the things of the Lord. *The International Standard Bible Encyclopedia*'s article "Disciples" states that in all cases a disciple is not only one who accepts the views of his teachers, but is also an adherent in practice.[3] Thus, in the widest sense of the usage of the word, it refers to those who accept the teaching of someone not only in belief, but also in practice. Ferrar says that the disciple of Jesus Christ today may be described as "one who believes his doctrine, rests upon his sacrifice, imbibes his spirit, and imitates his example."[4] Actually, there are two ideas that are inherent in the word *disciple*. Not only is a disciple a follower in the sense that he is following an individual or that individual's beliefs, but a disciple is also a learner. The noun form of disciple, *manthano*, means "to learn." A true disciple of the Lord Jesus Christ is not only one who is following His teachings and His practices, but one who is growing in grace and in the knowledge of the Lord.

Bill Crouch of the Sudan Interior Mission says that the greatest threat to the church in Africa is "the lack of teaching, and the consequent lack of maturity and understanding of Christian truth. To continue without a discipling program will increase the problem, especially if present trends continue and multitudes are added to the church and enter into the responsibilities of the Christian life without a knowledge of scriptural principles, and with little by way of experience on the part of older Christians."[5] I believe that what one of Africa's most experienced mission administrators is speaking of, regarding the church in Africa, is true of the church wherever it may be on planet earth.

The tragedy today is that we have thought that giving birth spiritually to babies, or making converts, is all that is involved in the process of making disciples. Even though it is possible to make a convert without making a disciple (in the sense that the person is growing to the place of maturity), it is impossible to make a disciple without first making a convert. Apparently the New Testament is saying to us that the discipling process is like a coin with two sides. The first side is the emphasis of the gospel, of evangelism, of the birth message, of obstetrics, of making converts, while the other side of the coin is an emphasis on the whole council of God—teaching, the growth message, pediatrics, and making disciples.

What is the procedure or process for making disciples? The latter part of verse 19 and the first part of verse 20 give to us the two-fold process of making disciples. The first participle is *baptizing*. As we have already stated, baptism was the outward testimony to both the saved and the unsaved world of the inner change and transformation that had taken place in the life of the new believer. Baptism was the means whereby the individual believer indicated his desire to be separated from the world and to be separated to Jesus Christ, and to be banded together with other believers of like faith. Thus, it seems that the New Testament is emphasizing that in the ordinance of baptism, believers were expressing their desire to fellowship together in what the New Testament calls the church.

The second aspect of the process of discipling is the process of teaching. Some time ago in a Sunday-school conference I quoted Matthew 28:20 in this fashion: "Teaching them to recite Bible verses and to pray theologically correct prayers, and to give correct answers to Sunday-school teachers. Amen?" To my amazement, I received an "Amen" in that particular workshop. I don't know who was more embarrassed, the person who said "Amen" or myself. The interesting thing to note, of course, is that verse 20 says we are to "teach in such a way that they may be able to observe all things, whatever our Lord gave command to us."

This actually is a reaffirmation of the truth that Moses gave to the children of Israel in Deuteronomy 6 just prior to their entering the Promised Land. The emphasis not only of chapter 6 but again and again throughout the book of Deuteronomy is "to teach, to do, to observe." The tragedy today is that we often teach so that our children and young people are only able to verbalize their Christianity when the emphasis of the Scriptures is not only that they must know something, but that they must be able to observe and do that which they know. Larry Richards is absolutely right when he emphasizes that not only must our students go through the process of rote but ultimately they must achieve the realization of the truth they have committed to memory.[6] Verbalization without actualization is not a fulfillment of the command of the Great Commission.

Finally, the Great Commission of Matthew 28 closes with a promise. Our Lord says, "And lo, I am with you until the completion of the age." The exciting thing to recognize is that our Lord had said in Matthew 16:18 that He was going to build "my church" and that the gates of Hades would not prevail against it. Earlier in the Great Commission of Matthew 28, He stated that "all authority has been given to me in heaven and in earth." I believe that He is giving to us the authority that we need to carry out the responsibilities that He has given. Not only has He given to us these two promises, but He closes the Great Commission by promising that He is going to stick with us until the job is completed. He is not only the one who started it, but it is His program and He is going to see it through to its completion.

What are some of the observations from the Great Commission passage of Matthew 28 that will help us to summarize the truth that our Lord has given?

The Great Commission was given to worshipers. The truth apparently that the Scripture is giving to us is that worshipers are workers. In the words of the Apostle Paul in 2 Corinthians 5:14, it is the love of Christ and our love for Him that impels, propels or motivates us to become involved in serving Him.

The Great Commission assumes that we have already gone. The question is not, "Should we go?" but, "What should we do?" Because of the response of worship, our Lord already knew that the disciples were sufficiently motivated, and His purpose in the Great Commission was to clarify the orders.

The Great Commission assumes that we are engaged in evangelism, making converts. He commands us to go beyond simply making converts to making disciples. It is possible to make converts without making disciples, but it is impossible to make a disciple without first reaching that individual with the message of the gospel.

The Great Commission is a command to teach, to edify. Believers are to teach all things that our Lord has commanded us, and we are to teach in such a way that the person will not only know what he believes, but will be able to practice what he believes.

The Great Commission includes a promise, a promise that our Lord is going to stick with the job until it is completed.

The Great Commission does become an imperative or command—not so much the command to go, but the command to make disciples.

The Great Commission, I believe, is best accomplished not through the hit-and-run type of teaching that is so often practiced in Christian education today, but through extended personal contact with people. It takes the impact of the life of a disciple in order to make a disciple, and this is not something that can be done strictly through cognitive learning and on the basis of short periods of time. Recognizing that the church today probably has a child only for 1 percent of his time, it becomes extremely doubtful as to whether or not the church with its present program will ever be able to truly make disciples. It seems then that the best place to make disciples is in the Christian home where the child spends 83 percent of his time and, in addition, also employ agencies like the Christian school where the child spends 16 percent of his time, or Christian camps where boys and girls and young people are able to spend long periods of time having contact with godly teachers, counselors, and staff personnel. Discipleship comes from relationships.

The second passage of Scripture containing the Great Commission is found in Mark 16:15. There is controversy regarding the ending of Mark 16:9–20 because several of the ancient manuscripts available do not contain these verses. First of all, let us assume that these verses are not a part of the original Gospel of Mark. If it is true that these verses were added later, then even though they would not be a part of Mark's original writings, they certainly would provide us an excellent second- or third-century commentary of what the church believed was their responsibility. However, it is just as clear to scholars that Mark did not intend to end his Gospel with verse 8, and though there are no first-century documents available containing these verses, they are well documented from second- and third-century writings.[7] Whether Mark 16:9–20 actually is a clear original statement of Mark himself or whether it actually is a second- or third-century commentary, the fact is that the debate continues and to this point has not been resolved by any available scholarship. Regardless, Mark 16:15 is worthy of our consideration as a part of the Great Commission passages by our Lord.

Again, it is important for us to note that the so-called command to "go into all the world" at the beginning of Mark 16:15 is in fact not a verb in the imperative or command form, but is actually a participle. In fact, it is the exact same participial form as found in Matthew 28:19 and thus would be much better translated as "going," or "in your going," or "having gone therefore." Again, we must be aware of the fact that the verb which follows the participle is in the imperative or command form, and once again the participial phrase can assume the characteristics or the qualities of the verb that follows it. Thus, one might translate Mark 16:15 as a command to go, but only if it is understood that the command to go is a weak command and that the main verb and the main thrust of the verse is found in the imperative which says "preach [or proclaim] the gospel."

An interesting point that probably ought to be made at this juncture is that the primary thrust of the Great Commission statement of Matthew 28:19, "make disciples," or "teach," seems to be the emphasis on the process of teaching and helping the individual to grow through the understanding of the Word of God, growing in grace and in the knowledge of the Lord. I recognize that if one said that the thrust of Matthew 28:19 is edification (education), this might be construed as a statement diametrically opposed to evangelism. But I believe that when Matthew 28:19 and Mark 16:15 are coupled, once again we have a coin with two sides that gives to us the perfect balance that only God and the Scriptures are capable of consistently giving to us.

The perfect balance would be that Mark 16:15 is primarily an emphasis on evangelism, of making the penetration into the lost world with the message of the gospel, with the purpose of confronting people with the claims of Jesus Christ, in order to bring them to a place of decision. The thrust of the other side of the coin as found in Matthew 28:19 is not to exclude the conversion or the evangelism aspect, but to move on into edification or the teaching or educational process of helping the individual to grow in the things of the Lord.

Certainly, one of the areas where there seems to be much confusion today in the evangelical church is in relationship to preaching. Often words that seem to be associated are *preaching, pulpit, pastor,* and *pew.* This particular pattern cannot be clearly seen either in principle or in specific illustrations in the New Testament. The issue, therefore, is not whether we should or should not be preaching, but rather that we need to understand who does the preaching, what they should preach, where they should preach, as well as to whom they should preach. Consider some biblical principles of preaching.

Preaching in the New Testament apparently was not done only by what we would call an ordained preacher or one called to the "professional ministry." In Acts 8, we find Philip involved in an extremely successful evangelistic campaign. Here he is preaching the gospel in spite of the fact that he was only one of the deacons chosen back in Acts 6. Philip not only preached in Samaria, but in Acts 8:35 he preached or proclaimed Jesus to the Ethiopian eunuch from the fifty-third chapter of Isaiah.

Preaching in the New Testament was not directed primarily for believers, but to the unsaved. In Acts 8:35 the message proclaimed was to one not yet "born again." Whether the ministry was from John the Baptist, our Lord, or others in the New Testament, preaching was primarily directed to the unsaved and not Christians. An interesting fact to note from the New Testament is that of the seventy-two references for the word translated "preach" or "proclaim," probably only one of them refers to preaching when it is being done with believers and unbelievers together. The fact is that only once in all of the New Testament is there mention of the unsaved being in the congregation with the believers as they are gathered together, and that is found in 1 Corinthians 14 in the context of speaking in tongues. The one reference that might be construed as relating to both believers and unbelievers is 2 Timothy 4:2 where

Paul is giving the charge to young Timothy regarding the various phases or aspects of his ministry. (*See* Appendix C.)

Preaching in the New Testament involved the simple gospel message and was not primarily concerned with the message of Christian living for Christian groups. The thrust of the gospel in the New Testament was the thrust of preaching: salvation was available for all who would believe. It is true that Paul speaks of the "whole gospel" which is the complete revelation of the truth of God, but when the New Testament writers spoke about proclaiming or preaching, they were speaking primarily about the gospel or the good news message.

It is rather interesting to take this concept and use it to compare the ministries of Jesus Christ and John the Baptist. As J. M. Price points out in his book *Jesus the Teacher,* though Jesus preached as well as taught, he is never referred to as "the preacher," but always as the "teacher." In striking contrast to the ministry of our Lord, we find that the ministry of John the Baptist apparently focused on proclaiming the message of repentance. Nowhere is John the Baptist referred to as "the teacher," but he is always referred to as "the preacher."[8]

Probably the clearest statement of the gospel is in 1 Corinthians 15:3, 4. "For I delivered unto you first of all that which I also received, how that Christ died for our sins according to the scriptures; and that he was buried, and that he rose again the third day according to the scriptures." Thus, preaching in the New Testament involved the proclamation of the simple gospel message, the good news of the saving grace of the Lord Jesus Christ.

Preaching in the New Testament did not involve pressuring people for decisions. Nowhere in the New Testament is pressure applied in order to get a decision. After a clear and logical presentation of the claims of Jesus Christ both on an intellectual as well as an emotional level, the individual was allowed to make his own "yes" or "no" decision. As one of my seminary professors would say, "I would rather have a man make an intelligent 'no' decision than to have him make an unintelligent 'yes.'" Apparently the aspect of making a decision in the New

Testament is something that was strictly in the hands of the Holy Spirit.

Finally, preaching in the New Testament allowed for only two possible responses. It was simply a matter of believing and receiving Jesus Christ as personal Lord and Savior, or rejecting the claims presented. In Mark 6:12 the writer states, "And they went out, and preached that men should repent." According to the New Testament, acceptance of the gospel produced new life, while rejection confirmed death and condemnation. Both the Gospel of John and the first epistle of John speak quite pointedly to this. John 3:18 states, "He that believeth on him is not condemned: but he that believeth not is condemned already, because he hath not believed in the name of the only begotten Son of God." Later John adds, "He that believeth on the Son hath everlasting life: and he that believeth not shall not see life; but the wrath of God abideth on him." In the "know so" chapter of 1 John 5 the writer states, beginning at verse 11, "And this is the record, that God hath given to us eternal life, and this life is in his Son. He that hath the Son hath life; and he that hath not the Son of God hath not life." Thus, believing is all that is involved in receiving Jesus Christ as personal Lord and Savior. As a result of this belief or faith, the individual will experience the truth of 2 Corinthians 5:17: "If any man be in Christ, he is a new [brand-new] creation."

On the basis of the New Testament, God's program for this age involves preaching (proclamation) and teaching, or evangelism and edification. Further, one can conclude that the work of the church, when God's people are gathered together, should be primarily to edify or to build them up. The work of the church scattered into the community is to preach or proclaim the gospel, the good news of saving grace in Christ Jesus. The focus of attention, then, in the church when the believers are gathered together should be teaching-edification, while the focus of the church when it is scattered into the community is preaching-evangelism.

The New Testament certainly does not demand that we stop preaching; on the contrary, it insists that every believer share the gospel. It also clearly tells us to preach or proclaim the gospel to the lost where they are. Preaching or proclaiming the gospel is God's means of bringing souls into sonship, while teaching or edification leads believers into discipleship. Preach the gospel? By all means— "for the harvest truly is plenteous," but preach the gospel to the lost where they are. "Ye are my witnesses, is the Lord's command. Ye are my witnesses; I have no other plan. How shall they hear and how shall they believe until the gospel they receive. For Christ said, 'Ye are my witnesses.' " Preaching the gospel is not a gift, but that which every believer should be doing; it is witnessing for Christ.

Luke 24:45–48 is the next Great Commission passage that must be examined. The occasion for this statement regarding the commission of our Lord is probably on the same day of our Lord's resurrection. The disciples were trembling behind closed doors, wondering what was going to happen next, and the Lord appeared in their midst. "Then opened he their understanding, that they might understand the scriptures, and said unto them, Thus it is written, and thus it behoved Christ to suffer, and to rise from the dead the third day: And that repentance and remission of sins should be preached in his name among all nations, beginning at Jerusalem. And ye are witnesses of these things."

Certainly the thrust of the statement of the Great Commission in Luke regarding the methods that would be employed was that of preaching or proclaiming the gospel. Also, as we have seen in both Matthew and Mark's Gospels, the scope of the emphasis of missions was to the world. There was no geographical or ethnic limitation regarding the spreading of the gospel message. Finally, the message that they were to proclaim was that of the gospel, the good news of saving grace in Jesus Christ. Our Lord's closing comment in verse 48 is the fact that they were "witnesses of these things."

The word *witness* in Luke 24:48 is the same as found in Acts 1:8. A witness was a martyr (*marturo*), but the word did not originally mean to die for what you believed. Actually, a martyr, in the sense that our Lord was using it, was one who lived for what he believed. The tragedy, of course, was that as a result of living on their convictions they lost their lives, and so later the idea developed that a martyr was someone who died for his faith.

If it is possible to make a slight distinction between the word *preaching* and the word *witness,* the distinction might be this. Preaching is the verbal witness or testimony of the gospel message; being a witness or martyr is living the life that would provide the visual back-up of the verbal witness. I think it is significant that here in Luke the words "preaching" and "witness" are used together. The initial idea was that repentance and remission of sins, or repentance unto remission of sins, was that which should be preached. But in order for this verbal witness to be given effectively, it would require individuals who were living the Christian life in an exemplary fashion.

Acts 1:8 is another occasion where we have a statement of the Great Commission. "But ye shall receive power, the Holy Spirit coming upon you, and you will be witnesses of me both in Jerusalem, and in all Judea, and Samaria and unto the extremity or the uttermost parts of the earth." The emphasis of Dr. Luke in the words that our Lord had given just prior to His ascension was not only that they were to be living witnesses or testimonies of the gospel of the Lord Jesus Christ, but the emphasis here is on the power, means, or ability to be able to be this witness that God intended them to be. Acts 1:8, in the construction of the original text of this verse, shows clearly that the receiving of power and the coming of the Holy Spirit upon the individual are things that happen simultaneously.

In other words, it is not a matter of receiving this power at a later time after one receives the Holy Spirit, or that one receives the Holy Spirit at a period of time after he becomes a born-again believer. The Scripture is very clear in Romans 8:9 that "If any man have not the Spirit of Christ, he is none of his."[9] Thus we can conclude that every believer in Christ in this age has the Holy Spirit. Also, from 1 Corinthians 6:19, 20 we can conclude that every believer in this age is continually indwelt by the Holy Spirit; and as a result of having the continual

indwelling presence of the Holy Spirit, every believer has this
potential for power. Whether or not the individual believer by
faith is drawing upon or appropriating that power is another
question, but the fact is that that power is resident in the life of
every believer as a result of the continual indwelling presence
of the Holy Spirit.

The scene for John 20:21 is probably the same as that
which we find in Luke 24. It is probably on the resurrection day
when the disciples were gathered in a state of confusion and
turmoil, and our Lord comes into their midst and says, "Peace
be unto you." In verse 20 He shows to them His hands and His
side, and His disciples rejoiced—not because they had seen His
wounds, but because they now knew that their Lord and Master, Jesus Christ, was truly alive. In verse 21 of chapter 20 our
Lord, without any commands at all, gives them the thrust of
what we know as the Great Commission. The authority in this
case is the Father, and our Lord says, "As the Father has sent
me, so I am sending you as my disciples, and those who will follow you. Peace be unto you, as my Father has sent me." This is
just the simple word (*pempo*) for "send." It is significant to note
that even though they did not ask for the power of the Holy
Spirit, nor probably did they fully understand what our Lord
had done, He breathed on them and said, "Receive ye the Holy
Spirit."

One further verse of Scripture needs to be considered as a
part of the Great Commission, and that is Luke 10:2. "Therefore said he unto them, The harvest truly is great, but the labourers are few. Pray ye therefore the Lord of the harvest, that
he would send forth labourers into his harvest." Our Lord is
saying to us that there will always be a tremendous potential for
a harvest of souls. The grain is white already unto harvest; there
is no lack of an audience or a lack of individuals who might potentially respond to the gospel. The problem is that there are
not enough workers to get out the message and reap the harvest.
The solution that our Lord gives is not that we should establish
more Christian schools in order to train more workers, as important as this may be, nor is it that we should establish bigger

or better programs of evangelism, but that we should pray to the Lord of the harvest that He would be the one to thrust forth the workers. This is the strong word for "send" (*ballo*, prefixed by the preposition *ek*).

This shows us that it is only the Lord of the harvest who can thrust forth the laborers into the harvest fields. It is also significant to note that it is *His* harvest field that the laborers are being thrust into. Our Lord has given to us the unique privilege of joining together with Him in a cooperative ministry. He is the one who thrusts us forth, and He thrusts us into, not our harvest field, but into His.

It is impossible on the basis of these Great Commission passages that we have examined to conclude that God's program is an either/or proposition. Though some are trying to make it either soul-winning or teaching, or evangelism or edification, yet on the basis of these passages God's program for this age is clearly a coin that has two sides. God's program for this age involves the thrust of preaching or proclaiming the gospel. This is in order to bring men and women, boys and girls to the place where they can make an intelligent response. However, we must not leave them at that point, but nurture them and help them to be edified or built up in the faith. Though there may be a difference of emphasis in terms of logical or chronological order, and though there may be a difference of emphasis in terms of geographical sphere, clearly the program of God for this age involves both the birth message as well as the growth message.

The New Testament is teaching us that the most important work of the church when it is gathered together is to teach or to edify or to build up believers. The church in the New Testament is not a soul-saving center, but a school. The tragedy is that some are only emphasizing that side of the coin. We must never lose sight of the fact that the most important work of the church when it is scattered back into the community is to make a penetration with the message of the gospel, so that those who are lost and without Jesus Christ may be able to make an intelligent response to the gospel. The most important work in the church is teaching-edification, while the most important work outside the church is preaching-evangelism.

There is nothing more wonderful than to see a baby born, but there is nothing more tragic than to come back some time later and discover that the little one has not grown. In many cases, this is a picture of what is happening today because we have not clearly understood the full spectrum of God's program for this age. In your going into all the world, proclaim the gospel. Give the birth message of salvation to those who need to be born into the family of God. But don't stop there. Give them the growth message. Teach them the "all things" that they need to know in order that they might become mature, reproducing disciples of the Lord Jesus Christ. When all fails, follow the instructions.

PART FOUR

Where Are We, and Where Are We Going?

9

Current Trends in Christian-School Education

Where are we, and where are we going? What are the educational flags that are being hoisted and the winds that are blowing that might help us gain a sense of perspective not only regarding the present, but also the future of Christian education?

Throughout the 1960s education was in the spotlight and the watchword was *change*. The decade of the seventies continued to bring us unprecedented change. The watchwords now are much more sophisticated because the word *change* became a highly emotionally charged word. Change to many implied that the old was bad and the new was good. And though in many cases neither was true, it was easy to split ranks right down the middle.

The new watchwords for the decade of the seventies discovered from searching the literature as well as observing the educational scene were three: *accountability, innovation,* and *relevance.* I am interested to note that the first letter of these three new watchwords spells the word *air,* which might give us some indication of the jumbled and yet sophisticated mess we face in education. Though there are three new watchwords, the one that continues to attract the most attention is *accountability.* Undoubtedly the force affecting change in education which is having the most tremendous impact in the eighties is accountability. While public education in the past has not been thought of as a competitive enterprise, the economic crunch and the rise of Christian schools has forced educators to give an answer. At present the citizens of the United States dig into their pockets for more than forty billion dollars each year to keep the educational machinery operating. Accountability will certainly require local school directors to establish priorities for expenditures, to reassess the utilization of staff, resources and housing, and finally to develop budgeting and accounting systems which will equate projected programs with price tags and productiveness.

With the current watchword of *accountability* as well as continual emphasis on innovation and relevance as we enter the decade of the eighties, what are the current signs rising on the elementary and secondary horizons? With no attempt at all to try to be objective, I believe there are generally ten areas where one can see the educational signs of the times in the broad spectrum of elementary and secondary education.

(1) Organization—Structure

In the area of organization or structural trends, the vertical organization of schools seems to be moving more to a 4-4-4 pattern. Many schools seem to be utilizing a middle-school concept, though not all schools and school districts are using these three precise four-year divisions. There does seem to be a shift at least to using the term *middle school* as opposed to the term *junior high school.* In the area of horizontal organization, there continues to be some movement in the direction of using the open concept as a means of achieving some degree of flexibility as well as nongradedness. There is an increasing desire, particularly in the social-studies area, to provide a family concept approach at the elementary level with heterogeneous multi-age-level groupings increasingly suggested in the curriculum literature.

(2) Administration

In the administration area, the watchwords seem to continue to be such terms as *decentralization,* allowing for a greater sharing of authority and thus necessitating a greater degree of delegated responsibility. The concept of administration used today believes that the decision for a particular problem can best be made at the point closest to the problem, thus encouraging a greater degree of decentralization of the administrative decision-making process. However, with the shared authority and responsibility comes the accountability, which is one of the prices paid for a chance to be a part of the decision-making process. In addition, there seems to be much less desire to have standing committees to deal in certain broad areas, but rather *ad-hoc* committees are used to deal with specific problems and tasks so that when these are completed the committees are immediately dissolved.

(3) Philosophy

The area of philosophy reveals quite a revival of the experience concept approach of John Dewey. His writings are again coming to the fore. Even the writings of John Amos Comenius (1590–1670), author of the great *Didactic,* seem to be having a slight revival as educators once again attempt to grapple with the content-experience and process-product concepts. It is Charles Silberman, in his book *Crisis in the Classroom: The Remaking of American Education,* who says that the great need today is to "provide teachers with a sense of purpose and philosophy of education."[1] Silberman believes that schools of education in America are not providing prospective teachers a singular purpose or consistent educational philosophy. Especially this is true for a philosophy integrated with the Truth of the Word of God and equipping one to be a teacher in a Christian school.

(4) Psychology of Teaching-Learning

In the psychology of teaching and learning, a great deal of emphasis is being placed on critical thinking. It was the Educational Policies Committee of 1962 which stated "the central purpose of education is to help students develop the ability to think." The work of Benjamin Bloom in his *Taxonomy* has certainly helped to create an awareness that much of education has been simply at the memory, rote, or recitation level. The work of Norris Sanders in the book *Classroom Questions—What Kinds?* goes a long way toward helping the teacher develop the kind of thinking that involves all of the processes above the memory level. Also, the work of Frank Ryan in his book *Exemplars for the New Social Studies* has facilitated the development of questioning strategies to implement the higher-order concept of critical thinking.

In addition to the trend of critical thinking, a great deal of work has been done in the nursery-school and early-childhood education. Particularly this is supported by the work of the "giant of the nursery school," Jean Piaget. Also, work on the open concept of learning has grown. This actually comes from the British open concept, developed more by necessity during World War II.

In addition, some writers are stressing the need for "control" for facilitating better learning. Obviously this would require greater discipline, and unfortunately the trend of society reflected in the laws of our land seems to provide more rights and freedoms for the students rather than the right of the teacher to establish educational and disciplinary standards.

The role of the teacher and the student also seems to be in the process of redefinition. Rather than the teacher being the dispenser of information, the teacher's role is now more of a facilitator attempting to motivate the student to become a part of the process rather than simply absorbing the product or the end result of the teacher's study. Some of this redefinition has been explained by the work of Thorndike and Skinner and the application of the principles of learning from behavioral psychology to the field of education.

Finally, in the area of psychology of teaching and learning, there seems to be a greater concern for the students' "moral and physical well-being" with a reemphasis on the development of the "total child." Though it is true that the spiritual areas still are relegated to the moral or aesthetic qualities, educators more and more reemphasize the necessity of dealing with the child as a total person rather than simply as an intellectual being.

(5) Curriculum

The curriculum area has seen an emphasis upon the delivery of the basic structure of the subject or discipline, and then teaching from this structure the basic concepts or principles. Writers such as Hilda Taba and Bruce Joyce have done much in the development of new forms, especially in the social-studies area. Along with the emphasis on teaching concepts rather than simply facts is also the development of teaching strategies. These strategies not only include the behavioral objectives, but also the content and the methodology along with the specific questioning strategies used to move the student off the memory level and on to the higher thought processes of critical thinking. Finally, emphasis on the use of multimedia has demanded a greater utilization of community resources. Martha Irwin and Wilma Russell, in their book *The Community Is the Classroom*, attempt to show how the community can become a multimedia resource center that is effective in preparing students to live in the world.

(6) Technology

In the area of technology, suffice it to say that there continues to be an expanding use of educational tools all the way from the cassette recorder to the video recorder, and now the additional availability of even the computer for teaching purposes. The strange phenomenon is that even though there has been an increased availability of hardware for educational use, there still is nowhere near enough software or programs and materials to in many cases encourage the teacher to more adequately use the educational technology that is at hand. The principle of availability being the key to usability continues to hold true in regard to the use of technology in education.

(7) Terminology

In searching the educational literature over the past twenty years, it was discovered that even though there are some new or expanded concepts the real trend is far more in the development of new or sophisticated terminology to express many of the concepts which have been around for a long time. For instance, the teacher who in the past was primarily looked upon as a lecturer is now said to be engaged in *expository teaching*. If this term were being used to describe the pulpit teaching ministry of a pastor, this probably would be considered a complimentary term. However, even though the term is not considered to be completely negative in its connotation, there certainly are negative overtones connected with it if the teacher is only talking or lecturing and carrying on one-way communication. A similar expression is the chalk-and-talk teacher, where the teacher is primarily talking and using only the chalkboard for visual communication.

With the work of Benjamin Bloom, the term *critical thinking* or *higher order of thinking* certainly has taken on great prominence. Though we recognize the importance of the memory or recitation step, we are aware that most of education in the past has started and stopped at this particular level. One place where this is particularly seen is in the fact that most of testing in the past was simply by a process of "rote, regurgitate, and reward." Bruce Joyce has termed the process of moving from one level of critical thinking to another as the process of modular cognition, while Jean Piaget talks of the problem of cognitive dissonance (that which takes place in the student's mind if he is not concretely involved in the process of moving from one level of critical thinking to another).

Terms such as *team teaching* have almost become obsolete in the current literature because they have been absorbed into the thinking of the "open concept" of education.

With the revival of the experiential approach to education of John Dewey, some of the new terms in the curriculum are *integrated curriculum, experiential curriculum,* or the *action-centered curriculum.* These new terms are attempts to show the necessity for translating the facts, concepts or theories of the classroom into real life. Educators today are recognizing, much as John Dewey did, that education or learning cannot be separated from real life.

Currently there is a great deal of talk about developing teaching strategies. This involves the entire area of teaching methodology, but also includes such things as the behavioral objectives, subject matter to be taught, as well as the approach to be used in communication. To a certain extent, there is a similarity between developing a lesson plan and developing a teaching strategy. As mentioned, one part of this strategy is the behavioral objectives to be achieved in the particular lesson or unit. Behavioral objectives are not objectives exclusively related to changing behavior, but are the observable, measurable results to be achieved from the teaching-learning process.

Another way to describe the term *behavioral objective* would be the operationally defined objective which would describe the specific operation that you desire the student to be able to produce or perform as a result of his involvement in the teaching-learning process.

(8) Research

One of the tragedies of the past in education is that sound research affecting the advancement of curriculum theory has probably had the least affect on change. The lack of respectable replicable research has been a tremendous obstacle to the advancement of educational concepts and ultimately to educational change. In many instances in the past, educators would conceive an idea and then set out to do educational research to support it. In most instances, they were able to give what looked like research support to their particular educational theory. Unfortunately their research was seldom able to be duplicated and has not always been valid and reliable. When research of an educational nature was done by business or industry, it generally was respectable because of its validity and reliability. This trend, however, is rapidly changing, and now there is the emergence of valid contributory research.

(9) Finances

In the past, it was felt that the quality of education in some areas of our country was not all that it should be because of the lack of available finances. Because of the tax base in some communities, one school district might have much more money to spend for each student's education than another district. Though it is true that a certain minimal amount always must be available, it has become increasingly apparent that quality education is not necessarily dependent upon the amount of money spent per student for their education.

Another area of great concern is equality of access to education. Not everyone has been able to afford to live in certain communities, and for that reason many students from lower socioeconomic strata have not been able to have equal access to some of the better schools or better educational programs. This, by the way, continues to be a problem for Christian schools because of the rising cost of tuition.

One final note on the matter of finances is the conflict between church and state or the use of state or federal money for private- or parochial-school education. Though the courts are gradually clarifying this issue and moving more and more in favor of no public funds being used for parochial-school education, it is becoming increasingly apparent that some means of providing monies for private- or Christian-school education will be an absolute necessity. Whether this will be in the form of outright grants, in the form of a tax break for parents who are paying tuition, or in the form of a voucher system where each student will have a specific amount of money made available for his education to be spent at any state-approved or accredited school, be it public or private, it seems that some financial-aid system will have to be worked out. More and more parents have become dissatisfied with the product of the public school and are beginning to send their children to private schools. Already school districts are providing parents and students with "alternative schools"; so the wheels are already in motion for providing new alternatives. With the growing number of schools, a mixed-bag pressure group of Catholics, Mormons, Lutherans, Baptists, Independents, and so on will more and more apply the pressure.

(10) Facilities

The final trend seems to be in the area of facilities. Though there continues to be some experimenting in school construction, overall school construction certainly is down, both because of the financial crunch, as well as the lowering of student enrollment. In many parts of the country, school districts have more facilities than they can adequately use. The watchwords in new school construction in the eighties continue to be as they were in the late sixties and seventies—*functional, flexible* and *adaptable*. Though certain features are still built into a facility for use with specific age groups or specific subject areas, a tremendous effort is now being made to see to it that buildings for educational facilities are not "locked in," so that they are incapable of easy modifications.

Current Trends in Christian-School Education

Without a doubt, the most rapidly growing area in Christian education today is the expansion of the Christian-school min-

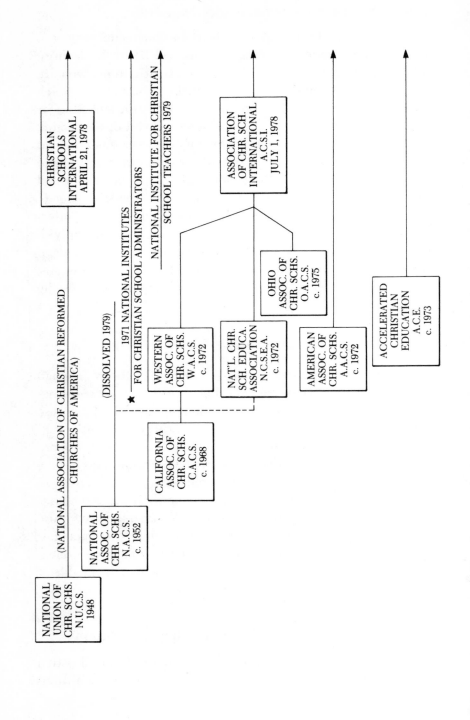

istry. What then are the current trends in Christian-school education? The Christian day-school movement has seen a *phenomenal growth in the number and size of Christian schools,* as well as the grades covered.

The California Association of Christian Schools started in 1967 with 102 member schools and 14,659 student enrollment. In 1972, when the name was changed to the Western Association of Christian Schools, it had grown to 246 schools and 34,949 students. Since the merger of the Western Association of Christian Schools, the National Christian School Education Association, and the Ohio Association of Christian Schools in 1978, there has been continued growth. As of January 21, 1980, the total schools had grown to 1,411 with total student enrollment at 228,080. In fact just a two-month update increases the member schools by 20 and the combined student enrollment by 7,913 (April 1, 1980—1,431 member schools, 235,993 student enrollment).

The National Institute of Christian School Administration, jointly sponsored by Grace College and Seminary and the Association of Christian Schools International, has seen a tremendous growth in the interest of the one-week summer institute program. In the summer of 1974, there were approximately 150 administrators representing over 24,000 students in Christian schools. By 1975, the institute had grown to 250 delegates even though there were over a dozen local or regional conventions each year. In the summer of 1979, an additional week was added (called the National Institute for Christian School Teachers), with the combined Administrators and Teachers Institute ministering to over 400 and growing to over 500 in the summer of 1981.

Unfortunately some Christian schools have been established in recent years as an *escape from the segregation and busing issues.* At first glance, this may appear to be strictly a regional or geographical problem. Apparently this is not the case, but is a problem faced to some extent throughout the entire United States.

While in the past many legitimately expressed concern regarding the academic level of Christian schools, today there seems to be a *steady rise in the competency level of Christian-school personnel,* both administrators and teachers. Though there may have been a time when Christian schools could be looked upon as providing a second- or third-rate education, and if a child attended he would suffer "an academic penalty," the educational level of Christian schools certainly is on the rise. While the testing of students in the public schools continues to indicate that in many parts of the country students are below the national norms, students tested in the Christian schools consistently are scoring above national norms.

A survey conducted by Dr. Paul Kienel, the executive director of the Association of Christian Schools International, confirms that an *increasing number of public-school educators are sending their children to Christian schools.* Though these men and women may be earning their living serving in the public school, they are increasingly aware of the problems of receiving a quality education, let alone being in an atmosphere that is even reasonably conducive to Christian growth. For these reasons, they are willing to spend the additional money for tuition to provide a Christian-school education for their children.

Though no specific answers seem to be available, at present there is an *increasing concern for state and federal aid to private- or Christian-school education.* In California there was a tremendous push for a tax credit for parents paying tuition for Christian-school education for their children. This, however, has been knocked down by the Supreme Court of the United States. Though the need is certainly apparent and the suggestion of either a tax credit or a voucher system seems to be closer to the answer, no specific decision has been made at this point. What has been made increasingly apparent is that there must be less and less involvement on the part of the public school in providing supplementary assistance to Christian schools. Special testing and reading programs, textbooks and even busing— it seems to be up for grabs as to whether or not the Christian schools will be able to retain any of these special services.

While so many Christian educators of the past seemed to be perfectly content to promote Christian education for the church, they have not always seen the necessity of a total education program for Christians based on God's revelation. Today, however, there is a *growing awareness that education based on any foundation other than that of God's revelation,* even though it may be the position of neutrality of the public school, *is not acceptable for Christians,* and is in fact atheistic in its educational position. Any philosophical system that is not avowedly theistic must be avowedly atheistic in nature. Dr. A. A. Hodge, the great theologian, in his special theological lectures in the 1890s, said, "The United States' system of national popular education will be the most efficient and widespread instrument for the propagation of atheism which the world has ever seen."[2]

Though it is true that any approach to Christian education which isolates children and young people from the world rather than insulating or preparing them to effectively face the world is not a valid form of Christian education, there is a *growing awareness that the "hothouse argument" is a strong argument for, not against, the Christian school.* Just as one does not take the tender young plant and place it in the garden to face the elements of the world until it is strong enough, so one should not place his children into the wrong hands until the children have the strength and personal convictions to be able to withstand the satanic forces or elements that are brought to bear upon them.

Since the inception of the public-school movement in 1850, the underlying philosophical basis has been one of neutrality. In fact, it was this problem that led Dr. Gordon Clark to say that the prayer of many who teach in the public-school system could very well be "O God, we neither assert nor deny thy existence; and O God, we neither obey nor disobey thy commands; we are completely neutral."[3] For the thinking Christian, it becomes increasingly apparent that it is impossible for anyone to be completely neutral or completely objective on any given subject. The Bible simply does not allow one to straddle the fence and take a position of neutrality.

The additional fact is that in reality, no person is capable of maintaining a completely objective or unbiased approach in anything that he does. Regardless of what philosophical position a person might take, it is this set of presuppositions that shades everything that the person thinks as well as does. In more recent years, as issues have surfaced in the public school, it is apparent that many of the public-school leaders not only cannot, but are not maintaining a position of neutrality. Again Dr. A. A. Hodge felt that what would happen if this position of neutrality were really followed was that "he that believes most must give way to him who believes least, and he who believes least must ultimately give way to him that believes absolutely nothing."[4] For this reason, there is a *growing realization that the public-school claim to neutrality is indeed a farce.*

There is also an increasing *realization that it is only the Christian school that is capable of dealing with and taking a stand on current issues such as discipline.* This also includes such issues as *dress codes, patriotism, sex education, values clarification,* and even the necessity for a quality educational program. A good education should equip a young person to be a functioning member of society; but when one looks at many of the graduates of our schools today, it is difficult to find those who have the moral and patriotic fiber to really be contributing members to our American way of life. A good Christian education, therefore, must not only equip a person to be a functioning member of society, but in addition a functioning member of the Body of Christ.

One final trend in Christian-school education today, which may not as yet be a trend but only a direction, is the *increasing proliferation of curriculum.* With the rapid growth of Christian schools, the demand for curriculum materials and packaged lesson plans has increased. Small schools with limited budgets have especially been hit hard and so have looked for legitimate alternatives. The heavy demand for starting schools, most of which will be small (less than fifty students to begin with) has also forced parents, pastors, and Christian-school leaders to seek approaches that are financially feasible with limited faculty and existing facilities. It is specifically the so-called individualized-instruction approach which has spread like a prairie fire, and therefore needs close attention.

At first glance, the problems and limiting factors associated with the traditional school are eliminated with the purchase of a packaged program. There is no question in my mind that these materials certainly can make a valuable contribution as supplementary materials, especially for the student who is highly motivated or somehow needs some special individualized attention. It is the philosophy behind this approach, not just the materials, that needs examination.

The problem associated with this packaged approach is that you are not always merely accepting a curriculum with the freedom to adapt it to each individual school, but in actuality you are accepting an entire philosophy of Christian education. While their materials may have a valuable contribution, this approach is based upon numerous potentially false assumptions. Only as these potential problem areas are honestly considered and adequately dealt with do I believe that this program is capable of providing any degree of quality education. Let's consider some of the misconceptions of this approach.

1. Every pastor is capable, with one week of training, yearly attendance at workshops, telephone consultations and field-representative assistance of handling the responsibilities of being a Christian-school administrator. Even though it is true that administration is a singular science, few if any pastors have been trained or are in any way adequately prepared to be an administrator of a local church, let alone an educational administrator in a Christian school.

According to Acts 6, Ephesians 4, and 1 Timothy 4, the pastor's primary responsibility is to give himself to a ministry of the Word and prayer. In fact, in Acts 6, church leaders did not feel that serving tables was inferior to their position, but they recognized that it did interfere with their primary responsibilities. Therefore, it was "not reasonable" that they should leave the primary and concentrate on the secondary. It would seem, then, that if pastors didn't have time to serve tables in the early church, it is not reasonable that pastors should leave the primary responsibility of ministering the Word and prayer to give leadership and direction to a Christian school.

In order to be effective as a Christian-school administrator, one must not only be trained biblically, but also a trained teacher and administrator. In other words, to be the most effective Christian-school administrator, one must be trained in the three disciplines of Bible, education and administration. The tragedy is that most pastors today are not only inadequately trained in the area of education, but the entire area of administration is conspicuously absent from the training programs of most Bible colleges and seminaries. Most pastors are not failing in the ministry because of their inability to handle the Word, but their inability to handle the administration or human relations problems that obviously are a part of every church or every organization.

2. The packaged-instruction approach does away with the need for the teacher in the classroom. Though there may not be precise educational research to support the conclusion, it has been generally agreed that what is being taught in any curriculum is less important than who is teaching. The most powerful influence upon the student comes from the personal model the teacher projects in the classroom. Some have concluded that the impact of the curriculum is only 10 percent, while the impact of the teacher is approximately 90 percent in the life of the student.

The teaching-learning process is a cooperative effort that involves not only the leading-guiding ministry of the Holy Spirit as seen in John 16:13, but also the leading-guiding ministry of the human instrumentality as seen in Acts 8:26–40 (especially verses 30 and 31). The same Greek word, *hodageo*, is used in both passages, helping us to understand that God seldom works apart from both the divine teacher as well as the human teacher. The human instrumentality can never be completely eliminated.

3. The students in the so-called individualized-instruction program, working at individual carrels, are equally, highly self-motivated. This implies that all students are potentially self-starters and that with only the written curriculum materials, the student brings to each session all of the built-in motivation necessary to make him an effective learner.

Interest and excitement for learning usually come as a result of the enthusiasm and excitement of the teacher as well as the teacher's ability to meaningfully involve the students in the learning process. As Dr. Howard Hendricks used to often remind us, "If you want your students to learn how to bleed, then you will have to learn how to hemorrhage." Actually what he is saying is, if you want your students to get excited about learning, then as a teacher you are going to have to get really excited.

4. Integration (relating Truth with truth and Truth with life) can be accomplished through the use of the printed curriculum materials without the use of teacher-to-student and student-to-student interaction. At best, the printed materials are probably capable of only producing correlation, laying one truth alongside another truth; but the ability to weave these concepts together into one piece of cloth, one concept, probably is the task of each teacher working with his or her students.

Probably most of what is being done today in the area of integration is only the first step of correlation. In correlation, you have the two concepts shown to be complementing one another and therefore not in conflict. In the complete process of integration, the two concepts have been woven together and have become one single, larger expanded concept. At the Truth-with-truth level, it is possible to correlate or integrate through the written materials; but ultimately, when the Truth/truth that is integrated at the theoretical level is integrated at the life level, this will have to be done by the teacher under the control of the Holy Spirit. Apparently, the control of the Holy Spirit gives to the individual the greatest potential for accomplishing the integrative process, not only in his own personal life, but also in the life of the students.

5. The students who are enrolled in the so-called individualized-instruction program work best at a study carrel interacting almost exclusively with a written or taped curriculum. Obviously the impact of the personality of the teacher is completely eliminated in the thrust of this program.

How did Jesus really teach? Was there just simply one single approach? What is the best approach to teaching and learning? Is it best to teach in large groups or small groups? Is it best to teach with two or three or even one on one? Is the best approach a self-contained classroom or some type of open-classroom concept? Is it best to teach simply in a classroom thirty feet by thirty feet, or is it best to teach using field experience? Is it best to use a homogeneous grouping of students, or is it best to use heterogeneous groupings with a mixture, such as the multi-age or multi-backgrounds type of situation? If we have learned anything at all from the study of education, it ought to be that there is no such thing as the "one best way" to always do things. In fact, generally you can write off any individual or group that says it has found "the answer." What he really means is that he has found his answer, in his situation, with his particular group of students. Probably, in actual practice, it could not be transferred to other groups. The principles may be transferred, but not the specifics.

Every one of the questions that we have raised could be shown to be a part of the teaching ministry of Jesus Christ. Apparently, in order to be effective as a teacher one must use a variety of approaches, for there is no singular best method or approach. Even though the truth to be taught is singular and the principles are cross-cultural, the technique, methodology, or organizational structure must be varied.

6. The students who are enrolled in the packaged-instruction program work best in a one-room schoolhouse environment (heterogeneous multi-age or grade group). Again, if we have learned one thing in education over the past years, it is that there is no one approach that is effective for every student in every situation. There is both a need for homogeneous as well as heterogeneous groupings, large groups as well as small group situations (see also point 5).

7. The responsibility for meeting the social and emotional needs through group involvement and interaction is not primarily the responsibility of the school (the total development of the child).

Group involvement and interaction on the part of the student is necessary in order to help prepare that student socially and emotionally to not only be a functioning member of society, but also a functioning member of the Body of Christ.

8. Any certified teacher, regardless of his grade-level or discipline specialization, is qualified to teach all grade levels and subject areas. The reason for this view is that it is felt the materials completely carry the student; and if the teacher does not know the subject area, then the teacher and the student together can work through the particular problem. As long as the teacher is born again, it is only recommended that he be certified.

Certainly all teachers in the Christian school must be born again, but they must in addition be certified and qualified teachers who are capable of articulating and implementing their philosophy of Christian education from a totally biblical perspective.

9. Parents, acting as monitors without the experience of actually working through the materials at each grade level or subject area, are capable of supervising a child's learning experience. These individuals are not functioning as teacher aides handling the administrative aspect of teaching, but are actually involving themselves in the teaching-learning process with the students.

If monitors in the program are acting as teachers, they must have the proper training in order to be properly qualified.

10. All churches are adequately equipped with state-approved educational facilities and minimal A.V. hardware for operating a school. All facilities must meet the reasonable fire safety, health and educational standards as required by the local, state, and federal governments. When it can be shown that the requirements are not really adding to the safety, health, and educational standards, then in most cases these items are negotiable with the fire marshal or the state inspector. However, as long as the Scripture says to "render to Caesar the things that are Caesar's," we must obey, unless these standards violate the clear commands or principles from the Word of God. To operate a school in violation in these areas, at least knowingly, is to knowingly be in violation of the Scriptures.

11. A single prepackaged plan without any local adaption of specified learning objectives or approaches is best for meeting the educational needs of all students throughout the United

States. In this case, we are not talking about adapting a curriculum guide, but are talking about adapting a specific program developed in detail, and there is no allowance for adaptation built into the program. Local adaptation may be assumed, but it is not recommended and certainly not encouraged in the packaged instruction program (*see also* point 1).

12. Any discrepancy between the so-called individualized curriculum and the state educational requirements or the locally designed curriculum guide simply shows the inadequacies of state and local educators to provide as high a quality program as the packaged program. This at least is an attitude often displayed.

The problem in points 11 and 12 relates to the problem of Christian schools following the prescribed curriculum requirements of the state. To what extent must Christian schools adhere to these prescribed standards? Again, let me emphasize that unless it can be clearly shown that some requirement is in violation of a direct command from the Word of God or a clear principle of it, then we must abide within the parameters that have been established by the state regardless of the area to which it pertains.

13. The so-called individualized-instruction program is not teacher centered, but learner centered—because "children love to learn, but they dislike being taught." This type of statement obviously indicates total misunderstanding of the teaching-learning process. See chapter 4 and the statements regarding the teaching-learning process from the ten basic concepts.

14. The packaged approach eliminates failure and boredom by eliminating unfair competition and locked-step learning restraints. Lessons learned from education as well as those given to us in the Scripture show that all education has failure. This is something that cannot be eliminated, and though we do not want to major on the failures we certainly need to prepare children to face the realities of life.

15. Though the packaged approach is not specifically programmed for individualized instruction, it is capable of provid-

ing an accelerated program of instruction for each child. At best, these materials are an advanced correspondence program. Because individual objectives are not written for the students and immediate reinforcement is not provided with each lesson, it is unfair to claim that the materials are individualized instruction. The term *individualized instruction* means something in educational terminology today. It would require a completely new definition to justify calling these materials an individualized-instruction program for children.

Though it may be true that all fifteen of the statements are not a part of the written philosophy, these statements do generally reflect the approach of the schools using this packaged approach in terms of the actual field implementation. Whether or not all of these false assumptions were intended, they seem to be inherent problems that are built into this approach and often quickly surface once the program is put to work.

Let me emphasize again that I have not said that a school using these materials cannot succeed. What I am saying is that the group that is going to start such a school will have to really work in order to prevent these potential problem areas from surfacing. It would seem that if such a school were going to get underway, using these fifteen points as a checklist would be a good means of preventing the school from stumbling into the pitfalls that could conceivably keep the school from ever achieving a quality program of Christian education.

Current Needs

Finally, what are the current needs that we continue to face in the Christian-school movement? Though there are basically two areas where we continue to falter, there are five specific areas of need.

Finances continue to be the number-one problem for Christian schools at all levels. The cost of providing adequate facilities and equipment for all phases of academic program, along with the ability to pay reasonable salaries in the light of today's inflationary economy, continues to pose a monumental problem for Christian schools. In the late fifties and the early sixties, many Christian schools were not even paying salaries at 50 percent of the level of public schools in their particular area. Some fifteen years later we have finally risen to the place where salaries are approximately 75 percent of public-school salaries. Apart from the fact that the teacher market seems to be flooded and the fact that in many public-school situations things have so deteriorated, we would still probably be having great difficulties finding *certified* and *qualified* Christian teachers.

The second major area of need continues to be in the area of Christian-school *philosophy*. Many schools have not taken the time to adequately think through the Christian philosophy of education, and as a result have for all practical purposes developed an educational philosophy that simply has a veneer of Christianity. There are probably two major contributing factors to the weakness in the area of developing a distinctive Christian-school philosophy. The first is the fact that many Christian schools have come into being as a reactionary movement against many of the negative influences of the public school. As a result, many parents and Christian leaders are simply trying to extract their children and young people from a climate which is not conducive to spiritual growth. Almost without realizing it, they find themselves fighting many of these issues even after the children or young people are placed into a Christian school. The result continues to be negative rather than positive, to be fighting rather than taking time to formulate a positive distinctive Christian-school philosophy.

A second contributing factor seems to be that many Christian-school teachers and leaders, though adequately qualified to accept their educational responsibility, lack the thoroughness of preparation in biblical and theological areas. The result is they seem to lack the ability to thoroughly integrate their educational thinking into a framework that is uniquely and distinctively Christian. Far too many Christian schools, from kindergarten to college, are simply secular institutions with Christian teachers. These schools at best are only quasi- or pseudo-Christian institutions.

Following naturally out of the first two needs in the area of Christian schools, there continues to be a tremendous need in the area of adequate personnel for Christian schools along with educational facilities that in some way are comparable to the educational facilities provided by the public school. The lack of available finances has obviously hindered the ability of Christian schools to take giant steps in this area. A recent illustration of this was the desire of a Christian high school to find an administrator. The lack of qualified Christian-school administrators caused them to offer a salary to a qualified individual of from $18,000 to $25,000 per year. When they found the available administrator, they paid over $22,000 for this man's first-year salary, even though they were paying less than $7,000 per year for starting teachers. Though there seems to be a large number of certified teachers available who are Christians, there is still a need for teachers who are uniquely prepared for a ministry in the Christian day-school movement because they have developed a distinctive Christian philosophy of education that permeates their educational activities.

Because the Christian day-school movement is undoubtedly the most rapidly expanding area of Christian education today, there is a tremendous need for certified and qualified Christian-school administrators who are trained not only as teachers and as administrators, but also have a sufficient biblical and theological orientation to allow them to develop a distinctively Christian philosophy of education. There continues to be a grave danger in attracting to the Christian school experienced public-school administrators without providing reorientation and training for their new roles.

In the eyes of many parents desirous of sending their children to the Christian school, the level of quality of the Christian school is often judged by the quality of educational facilities and programs that are being provided. Many schools today are providing excellent first-rate new facilities, while many continue to use the existing educational facilities of a church or the discarded educational facilities of the public-school district of their area. This problem is being met by churches now beginning to build church educational facilities which are also more than adequate for a Christian day school.

The second area is that in some cases public-school districts are finding with the shifting population and dropping enrollments they are forced to consolidate programs and may discover that they have an adequate educational facility they no longer need. A Christian school in Grand Rapids, Michigan, beginning in the fall of 1975, began purchasing one of the finest facilities in the Grand Rapids area from the public-school district because the district no longer had need for this particular building.

The final area of need continues to be in the area of textbooks. The development of an adequate curriculum for K-12, along with texts that are academically sound and distinctively Christian, continues to pose a problem. Basically there are two approaches that are being taken. One is the use of secular textbooks, in order not to completely isolate the children and young people from the exposure of the thinking of the world. This of course requires the unusual ability of the teacher to integrate (interpret and orient) whatever the author is saying to a biblical perspective. The second approach completely discards all secular textbooks and uses materials that are either teacher- or school-prepared, but may be, though more Christian in their orientation, academically inadequate. The lack of ability on the part of Christian schools to cooperate in the massive endeavor of publishing Christian-school textbooks and materials has also hindered the ability of any one group to dominate the textbook publishing business. Today the cost of writing and publishing materials is astronomical, and though many have complained about the problem of obtaining academically sound and distinctively Christian textbooks, few have done anything about it. In an effort with the Association of Christian Schools International, a Christian School Textbook Advisory Board has been formulated and already dreams and ideas are becoming a reality in the form of quality curriculum guides, textbooks and supplementary materials for Christian schools.

10

Developing a Plan for Rethinking Christian Education

Charles Silberman wrote a controversial volume, *Crisis in the Classroom: The Remaking of American Education,* in which he stated that the great need in our schools of education is to "provide teachers with a sense of purpose and philosophy of education."[1] Because there is a lack of singular purpose or consistent philosophy even in Christian education, there is a crisis in our Christian schools and a need to rethink our approach to Christian education. In a broad sense, that has been the purpose of this entire presentation. However, drawing upon the suggestions and insights of specific chapters, the following plan is offered to assist in the process of rethinking Christian education as it relates particularly to our schools.

1. Acceptance of God's plan for this "age" as the building of His church and God's program as discipling involving a twofold thrust of proclaiming the gospel and teaching (evangelism and education). See chapters 1 and 2.

2. Acceptance of a theory of teaching-learning consistent with biblical and educational principles that demands a balance between teaching content (facts–concepts) as well as providing opportunities for experience (implementation or developing a high level of personal and professional competence). This is content–experience, concept–competence. See chapters 3 and 4.

3. Implementation of a program to immediately instruct all teaching faculty to the full ramification of a concept-competence curriculum both in classroom instruction as well as in the development of new courses and programs. See chapters 4 and 7.

4. Provide adequate training or retraining for all faculty to fully equip them to all be able to teach within the framework of a concept–competence curriculum. Total acceptance of this philosophy and its implementation would of necessity be within the span of a two- to three-year period. See chapters 3, 7 and 8.

5. With the emphasis now in the direction of a concept–competence curriculum, greater flexibility is required in the calendar organizational structure and classroom scheduling. The optimum of greatest flexibility is in modular scheduling using ten-, fifteen-, or twenty-minute blocks of time for daily class scheduling and weeks in place of semesters. Potentially this would allow for ten to twelve mods of three- to four-week lengths in each school calendar year. A suggested breakdown of the school calendar year for especially junior high through college would be seven weeks—one week—seven weeks—three or four weeks—seven weeks—one week—seven weeks and then summer school of two-, three- or four-week blocks.

6. Because of the necessity of developing competence as well as concepts, Christian service would need to be expanded to include not only a regular weekly involvement in ministry (possibly for credit) with close supervision, but would also require three or four months of both exposure as well as actual experience in the area of the vocational major for the student at the college or seminary level. This of necessity would be a requirement within the scope of every recognized major.

7. Convinced that every believer has at least one spiritual gift given for the purpose of contributing or ministering to the Body of Christ, the responsibility of the Christian school is therefore not to *dispense* spiritual gifts, but to guide students in the *discovery* (desire, other Christians helping you recognize it, God blessing it), *development*, and ultimately the *dedication* of these spiritual gifts.

Summary

Though the Bible college and seminary are distinctive in their basic philosophy and unique program of vocational training, the distinctive mark of excellence of all Christian education is the student who has discovered and developed his or her spiritual gift(s) and has dedicated them either in a lay or professional ministry for the fulfillment of the Great Commission. Thus, in the final analysis the distinctive mark of excellence of Christian education is its product, graduates who are capable of contributing significantly in strategic ministries wherever geographically God's "good, acceptable and perfect will" may lead them. The goal of Christian education is to equip the individual to be both a functioning member of society as well as a functioning member of the Body of Christ.

11

Developing Excellence in Christian Education.
So What? A Final N.B.

Where do we go from here? It seems to me that excellence in Christian education must ultimately be achieved by developing Christian educators who strive for excellence in personal growth, practical growth, and professional growth.

Personal Growth

The first item of concern in the area of personal growth is that the Christian educator must be filled (controlled) with the Word of God. These are desperate days of conflict in relationship to the authority and inerrancy of the Word of God, and Christian educators need to clearly declare themselves in relationship to the centrality of the Word of God. Almost more than being known as educators, the Christian educator today must be known as a man or woman of the Book. Second Timothy 2:15 does not primarily emphasize the command to "study" as much as it emphasizes what our attitude toward the Word of God should be. The verse says that we should "Be eager to show ourselves approved unto God, workmen who need not to be ashamed, rightly dividing the word of Truth." Certainly our eagerness to be approved demands not only a thorough study of the Word of God, but as good workmen we must approach the Word of God using good methods. The end result is that we will not be ashamed as we are able to rightly handle the Word of God.

Secondly, the Christian educator must be filled (controlled) with the Spirit. Ephesians 5:18 is clear when it states, "Be not drunk with wine, but be continually filled or controlled by the Holy Spirit." The Apostle Paul is saying that we should not be drunk with wine in the sense that we never even allow it to get started; but in striking contrast we should be allowing the Holy Spirit to continually fill or control our lives.

It is true that in most instances when the Scripture mentions being filled with the Holy Spirit, the emphasis immediately following is on something related to verbal communication. However, there were demonstrations of action, things the individual(s) did that occurred either before, during, or after the speaking but always in relationship to being filled with the Holy Spirit. Actually the fruit of the Spirit is love, and this *agape* love could involve verbal expression, but it demands action. *Agape* love involves the will, is not motivated by "what can I get" but "what can I give," and is willing to give and give even though it knows it will receive nothing in return. All of the other eight qualities (joy, peace, longsuffering, kindness, goodness, faithfulness, meekness [strength under control], self-control) could as well be demonstrated in a person's manner of speech, but would best be shown in the manner of living, the actions of the individual.

Part of our problem in understanding the concept *filling of the Holy Spirit* is that Paul in Ephesians 5:18 uses the analogy of being drunk. He does not say, however, "stop being drunk," the kind of Greek construction he uses in Ephesians 4:30—"stop grieving the Holy Spirit"—or in 1 Thessalonians 5:19—"stop quenching the Holy Spirit." What he is saying is: "Be not drunk with wine in the sense that you never even let this thing get started." I'm only using this as an illustration and in no way am I somehow endorsing drinking or drunkenness. But what does the analogy mean?

Dr. Daniel Noonan, a medical doctor from the University of Illinois, in discussing alcohol and drug use states that the thing that happens to persons in the first level of being drunk is that they lose their inhibitions. He illustrates by explaining that a salesman who is uptight could be helped while a pilot who has to make precise, split-second judgments would be hindered through alcohol use. However, we must hasten to add that the medical doctor warns that a person could become dependent on alcohol and without realizing it become an alcoholic. I think the general agreement would be that a person's speech is the first thing affected when he loses his inhibitions.[1]

Thus, when a person is controlled by the Holy Spirit, he also loses his inhibitions; but rather than the results being negative, the works of the flesh, they are positive, the fruit of the Spirit. Apparently Paul is telling us that as believers in the Body of Christ, we need to lose our inhibitions, become untied, loosed, set free by the power of the Holy Spirit.

The last thing that happens to a person when he is totally drunk is that he loses his integrative ability. Dr. Noonan explains it this way. The person who is normally a very moral, ethical, upright individual, now because he is totally drunk, loses his ability to make a transfer of his attitudes, values and standards from one area to another.[2] I believe that the person who is controlled by the Holy Spirit is the individual with the greatest potential for integration. This obviously is not some automatic process but apparently the potential is available.

What we desperately need in Christian education are teachers who because of the ministry of the Holy Spirit have lost their inhibitions and are able to develop warm, friendly, caring personal relationships with students and have gained the greatest spiritual enablement to integrate truth with Truth and ultimately Truth/truth with life.

Regardless of whether you translate the Greek preposition in Ephesians 5:18 or Galatians 5:16 as "in" (in the sphere of) or "by" (by means of, an enablement of the Holy Spirit), the fact remains that it must be the work or ministry of the Holy Spirit.

Recently I was watching as someone was buying some tropical fish at the store. The clerk took the fish from the tank and put them in a plastic bag filled with water. She then blew into the sack and tied it shut. The question then is, what difference does it make whether the fish is just swimming around in the bag (in—locative—sphere) or if he lies at the bottom of the sack (by—instrumental—by means of)? The important thing is only that the fish must be in the plastic bag. The important thing is that every believer has all the Holy Spirit (Romans 8:9; Galatians 4:6—Holy Spirit = Spirit of Christ) all of the time from the moment of conversion (1 Corinthians 6:19—temple = holiest of holies).

Some believe that because the "filling of the Holy Spirit" relates to speech and not actions, you cannot connect Ephesians 5:18 with Galatians 5:16. Though I agree that speaking is probably the first area affected when a person is drunk either with alcohol or with the Holy Spirit, the context of the passages relating to "filling" are not limited to speaking.

Ephesians 5:18–21 is really all one sentence, and following the "filling" of verse 18 there is the "speaking" in verse 19 and "giving thanks" in verse 20. However, in verse 21 there is an action described—we are to "submit" ourselves to one another. More specifically the verses that follow beginning at verse 22 and going at least to 6:4 give to us the roles and relationships of family members.

Another example of this is Saul (Acts 9:17–20). In verse 17 he is "filled," in verse 18 he receives his sight and is baptized, and in verse 19 he eats and is strengthened, remaining with the disciples. Finally, also in verse 20, he proclaims Christ in the synagogues. I definitely believe that the filling of the Holy Spirit not only affects my speech, but my whole manner of living. Galatians 5:16 states then that we should walk, taking each and every step by faith, by means of the Holy Spirit; then we will not fulfill the lusts of the flesh. The Apostle Paul in 1 Corinthians 2:15 has made it very clear that the spiritual person—that is, the individual who is filled or controlled by the Holy Spirit—has the ability to examine or differentiate all things. This is specifically in relationship to the Word of God, but I believe it also applies to "all truth."

Finally, in the area of personal growth the Christian educator must be balanced. Ephesians 4:1 says that the believer is to walk worthy or worthily of the calling. The Greek word for *worthily* is the picture of a balance beam, and apparently Paul is using it to indicate that a worthy walk is a walk that is in equal weight with or in balance with what the individual knows regarding the truth of the Word of God.

It is significant to note that the Apostle Paul makes reference to the word *walk* only twice in the first three chapters of the book of Ephesians. The first time is in reference to the former walk of the believer (2:2), while the second is in reference to the future walk of the believer (2:10). Apparently Paul's emphasis in chapters 1–3 is first of all on the believer's position, seated with Christ in the heavenlies, and then he emphasizes that the believer needs to learn to stand in this position in Christ. It is only after the believer has learned how to stand that Paul then emphasizes the believer's walk, but it is to be a walk that is in balance with what the person knows now regarding his exalted position seated with Christ in the heavenlies.

J. M. Price, the great Southern Baptist educator, says in his book *Jesus the Teacher,* "Jesus lived the truth more than He was able to teach it."[3] The problem of course for us is that we can teach the truth far more than we are able to live it. The danger that must always be guarded against is that our knowledge level must not greatly exceed our ability to experience the Word of God that we have come to know. As the believer stands before the judgment seat of Christ, the Apostle Paul tells us in 2 Corinthians 5:10, we are going to be judged on the basis of what sort of life we are living, but always in relationship to the truth from the Word of God that we know. The judgment apparently is on the quality of life in relationship to the quantity of truth from the Word of God to which we have been exposed.

Practical Growth

Certainly every Christian educator recognizes that the laboratory for our ministry is in our home (where we live). It is relatively easy to teach the truth of God's Word in a classroom situation, but the real test comes in whether or not we are able to live the truth of the Word of God before the other members of our family in our home. Without a doubt, the home is where the heart is revealed. In the pressure-cooker situation of your family life, the real you will always surface, and you find yourself completely exposed and bare as you stand before your loved ones in your family. Dr. Henry Brandt often publicly says that "circumstances don't make you, they reveal you," and this certainly would be true of the family situation in the home.

Whatever a Christian educator does, he must come to grips with the fact that his home is not essential to his ministry; it *is* his ministry. I believe that for all practical purposes, to fail in the choice privilege and responsibility that God has given us to minister to our families in our home is to fail in the ministry of top priority that God has given us. Every command of Scripture that relates to the nurturing or training of children has been given to parents, and often specifically to fathers. And now abides the church, the school and the home, these three, but the greatest of these is the home.

Professional Growth

The Apostle Paul has given to every Christian educator a behavioral objective that is worth striving for. Philippians 3:13, 14 says, "Brethren, I count not myself to have apprehended [to have laid hold of]: but this one thing I do, forgetting those things which are behind, and reaching forth to those which are before, I press toward the mark for the prize of the high calling of God in Christ Jesus." Certainly every Christian educator needs to be pressing toward the mark of improving or upgrading his professional competency.

Let's take the word *press* and use it as an acrostic for five suggestions for improving our professional growth. First of all, *professional organization.* Certainly every Christian educator ought to give serious consideration to the professional organization that specifically relates to his or her field. This is an excellent means of keeping abreast of what is happening in the field as well as providing interaction with other professionals.

The second area is *reading.* This, of course, is not only reading in the area directly related to your particular field, but also in related areas that will sharpen your abilities as a professional educator and keep you on the cutting edge of what is happening in your field.

Thirdly, *educational advancement.* Certainly there are seminars and possibly even summer-school or extension classes available from Christian colleges, seminaries, the university or community college that can provide you with possible advancement in your field. Again this would not only be in relationship to an advanced degree, which certainly will be invaluable, but also to provide you with the fresh update in relationship to the field of Christian education.

Fourthly, *seminars and conferences.* There are many of these that are being held today, such as the National Institute for Christian School Teachers and Administrators, and it would be well for every Christian educator to participate in at least one professional-growth seminar annually. It is easy to find yourself constantly giving out without taking the time to be professionally filled or updated yourself; so these seminars can be invaluable.

The fifth and final area is simply personal *study.* This obviously requires a great deal of discipline, but regardless of what it takes it must be done. This would not only be study in relationship to educational concepts, but I find that often Christian educators, even though they do not neglect a more devotional study of the Word of God, often fail to take the time to really study and come to grips with the truth of the Word of God not only for their own lives personally, but also for their discipline or professional ministry.

First Corinthians 15:58 gives us a final summary of the kind of suggestion that I have been trying to put forth. "Therefore, my beloved brethren [in the ministry of Christian education], be ye stedfast, unmoveable, always abounding in the work of the Lord [in Christian education], knowing that your labor [in the glorious ministry of Christian education] is not in vain or empty."

So what? Where do we go from here? Christian educators must continue to strive for personal, practical and professional growth in order that we might be able to fulfill the principle given to us by the Apostle Paul in 2 Timothy 2:2: "and the things that thou hast heard of me among many witnesses, the same commit thou to faithful men [men who are full of faith], who shall be able [competent] to teach others also." Are you personally striving for competency as a Christian educator? I believe on the basis of the Word of God that this is something that is not optional, but absolutely imperative.

Appendix A

The Voice of the History of Christian Education Speaks

O you who claim to follow the One True God,
    you who have taken hold of the name of Jesus Christ,
    Hear the words I speak to you
        and understand what they say.
You who say you have The Truth,
    yet you cannot communicate it
        because of ignorance of it,
        lack of confidence in it,
        and fear of its possible power in you,
    Listen as I reveal what you have been
            and are
                and will be.

At the beginning the One True God intended that Life
    be constituted of learning;
    a process of learning who He is and of learning
        and growing in our relationship to Him.
He instituted the home as the base of educational operations.
    Parents were to be examples to their children,

children were to be able to watch, listen,
and imitate with complete confidence and respect.
But some of these parents did not accomplish their responsibility.
Actually *most* of them failed—
leaving a multitude of unlearned children
who congregated together in cities and places
and bequeathed their ignorance to each succeeding
generation.

Great leaders of the Faith in the One True God
became greatly concerned about the lack of knowledge
of the One True God in the lives of their people.
Steps made to counteract this creeping paralysis of ignorance
led to the formation of schools, places of learning
apart from the home.
Emphasis was placed upon the Word of the One True God
but soon the power of organization caused these leaders
to teach only their ideas, their laws,
and again the multitudes were left in ignorance
of the Word of the One True God.

As the pendulum of time swings steadily through the centuries,
so do the minds of men swing and change position.
Words, Reason, and Logic are stressed as it swings to the right,
but as it makes its way to the left
Feelings, Experience, and Mysticism come into view and
soon fill the whole scene.
The proponents of both extremes of the pendulum
claim that they are educating the people,
yet nothing is changed, and
with true education there must be change.

You who are called Christian,
who desire to reach the people today,
to teach and to train in order to bring about change in lives,
You must jump off of the swinging, swaying wisdom of man
and stand firmly on the Truth of the One True God
which, like a dial, never moves, but reveals all
by the Light of the Son, and will forever remain the same.

The mind of man will never discover the Truth.
It is bent
and no matter which way you turn it
it will always point away from God.

Today you must drop away from those patterns which keep you
away from the Word of the One True God
And you must dare to teach clearly His Truth
concerning what Life really is.

Listen, you educators called Christians,
    someday the pendulum of time will stop
    and if you have persisted in hanging on as other men
        listening to the words of men rather than the Word of God
You will slide off in the presence of God
            heavyhearted,
            empty-handed,
            and dizzy headed.

You do have the Truth,
    and it can set you free
        and multitudes of others after you,
If you will only release the grasping hold
    you have on the hand of those born blind.

JUANITA WRIGHT

Appendix B

The Bible Words That Focus on the Teaching-Learning Process

Old Testament Terms:

1. *Lamath* is the most common word for "teaching, learning." The word does not mean a dumping of facts, but a stimulation to imitation or action. This kind of learning means to become experienced; it means to become accustomed to something new, subjective assimilation.

Deut.	5:1	2 Sam.	1:18
			22:35
	31:13	Psalms	32:8
	4:10	Isaiah	25:9
	31:12	Jeremiah	31:34

2. *Be-en* basically means "to separate." It came to mean "distinguish." Learning is not a body of facts transferred like merchandise, but is differentiating, drawing conclu-

sions, stepping from truth, divining, distinguishing, discriminating.

Psalms 139:2	Psalms 19:12	
Daniel	9:23	Job	6:24
	10:1	Neh.	8:7
Prov.	23:1		8:8

3. *Alaph* originally meant "to cleave to." From this developed the idea of teaching by exposure or making something so familiar that you adopt it or hold on to it.

   Prov. 22:25   Job 33:33   Job 35:11

4. *Yah-dag* is to know by experience or by one's own observations—a highly subjective knowing or taking note of
   things.

Gen.	19:35	Judges	8:16
Josh.	23:14	Prov.	9:9
Exodus 10:2		Exodus 18:20 shew
2 Sam.	7:20, 21	Psalms 16:11 shew

5. *Dah-var* is the simple word "to speak, say or proclaim." It
   can mean to teach by simply speaking.

   Jer. 28:16.

6. *Yah-rah* means "to cast, throw or shoot." From this comes
   the idea of directive teaching. The word means "to point
   out" or "to direct one in a new path."

Gen.	46:28	1 Sam. 12:23
Exodus	4:12	Job	6:24
	4:15	Psalms 27:11
	25:12		119:33

7. *Za-har* originally meant "to shine or illuminate." Later
   came to mean "teach." Ignorance is darkness, knowledge
   is light. This is the word "teach" in Exodus 18:20. It is also
   translated "warn" in the sense of throwing light on a
   problem or on sin.

   Psalms 19:11   Daniel 12:3   Ezekiel 3:20

8. *Chah-cham* is the word that means "to be wise, intelli-

gent." Wisdom to the Jew was the ability to use facts in daily experience, applying doctrine to practical needs.

Prov.	6:6	Deut.	32:29
	8:33	Job	35:11
	23:19	Psalms	105:22
	27:11	Prov.	30:24

9. *Sah-chal.* The root idea is to show oneself very attentive, to look at and ponder or consider. The one who looks at something close enough gains insight. He becomes skilled in the subject.

Prov.	17:2 wise	1 Sam.	18:30 behaved wisely
	19:14 prudent	Prov.	16:20 wisely
	21:12 wisely considers	Dan.	1:4
Dan.	1:17 skill	Amos	5:13 prudent

10. *Shah-nan* means "to sharpen or whet," to whet the appetite or senses for learning. Used only once in this didactic sense, but then most graphically. "You shall sharpen your children's minds, cut deep into their understanding that they may know me . . ." (Deuteronomy 6:7).

11. *Rah-ah* literally means "to see," came to mean to consider carefully even to the point of seeing a need and making provision. To be a learner in this sense is to be one that looks carefully at a situation and learns by his observations.

Exodus 33:13 consider	Prov.	6:6 consider
Gen. 22:8 will provide	Num.	22:41 might see
2 Kings 9:17 spied	Judges 13:21 appear

New Testament Terms:

1. *Didasko* is the most common word for "teaching." The focus is on the activity of teaching.

Ephesians 4:21   1 Timothy 4:11
Colossians 1:28   6:2
           3:16   2 Timothy 2:2
2 Thess.   2:15   Titus   1:11

2. *Paideuo* means "to give guidance, instruct, train." It is
    used in the sense of raising a child. It can also refer to the
    corrective or disciplinary aspect of education. The verb
    comes from the noun that means "a little child."

Acts	7:22	learned	2 Tim. 2:25 instructing
	22:3	taught	Titus 2:12 teaching
1 Cor.	11:32	chastened	Heb. 12:6 chastens
1 Tim.	1:20	may learn	Eph. 6:4 nurture them in the discipline and admonition of the Lord

3. *Noutheteo* means "training by word of encouragement,"
    but can take a negative meaning as well of "reproving."
    Literally, it means "mind shaping." The noun is translated
    "admonition."

1 Cor.	10:11	admonition	1 Cor. 4:14 warn
Eph.	6:4	admonition	Col. 3:16 admonishing
Col.	1:28	warning	

4. *Katekeo* is "the giving out of information, of communicat-
    ing fact, or reporting, informing." It means to teach orally
    in regard to the elements of religion, to din into the mind.
    From this comes our word *catechism*.

Luke	1:4	instructed	Romans 2:18 being instructed
Acts	18:25	instructed	1 Cor. 14:19 might teach
Acts	21:21	informed	Gal. 6:6 taught, teacheth

5. *Matheteuo* means "to make a disciple" and implies in-
    struction with reference to loyalty and devotion. The
    Greek word for *disciple* is built from this root. The noun
    and the verb are not used in the epistles, only the Gospels.

    Matt. 28:19

6. *Oikodomeo* is the simple word "to build." Metaphorically, it means "to edify" and "edification." It is used in the contexts promoting spiritual growth and maturity. Both noun and verb are listed below.

   1 Cor. 8:1 edifies   1 Thess. 5:1 edify
   1 Pet. 2:5 built up   1 Cor. 3:9 building

7. *Manthano* means "to learn by practicing, experiencing, and doing." "Learn, appropriate to oneself less through instruction than through experience or practice."

   Heb. 5:8 Phil. 4:11 Matt. 11:29 9:13 Eph. 4:20

8. *Paratithemi* is to "put something before someone" in the sense that they mentally grasp it, "to place beside, set before."

   Matt. 13:24 Christ "put forth" His parables
   1 Tim. 1:18 committed
   2 Tim. 2:2 commit

9. *Ektithemi* means "set forth, expound, to explain" the facts in logical order—a defense of doctrine, a recital of facts, a narrative. Used four times in Acts only. Translated "expound."

   Acts 11:4 rehearsed
       18:25 explained
       28:23 set forth, expound

10. *Diermeneuo* means exclusively "to translate" or "interpret." From this we get our word *hermeneutics*, which in turn is derived from *Hermes*, the messenger of the gods. In Scripture this word refers to an "unfolding" or "opening" up of spiritual truth.

    Luke 24:27 interpreted

11. *Dianoigo* refers to God's process of opening the mind and heart to spiritual truth. Six of the eight uses in Scripture refer to God or Christ opening ears or eyes—scriptural meaning, hearts and understanding.

    Mark 7:34 Luke 24:32
          7:35   24:45
    Luke 24:31 Acts 16:14

12.   *Suniami* means "to comprehend, gain insight, put facts together for usefulness and to completely understand." A key passage is Ephesians 5:17. Paul tells the believer to put together certain biblical facts and arrive at an understanding of God's will for his life, developing biblical concepts.

13.   *Hodegeo* means "to lead or guide, to lead or cause one to discover practical doctrinal truth." The Spirit of God *guides* believers to understand spiritual truth (John 16:13); the Ethiopian desired someone to *guide* him into scriptural discernment (Acts 8:31); and Christ *shall lead* saints to experience living waters (Rev. 7:17).

14.   *Anangello* means "to report, proclaim or declare." It is used in reference to official declarations or reports. The Spirit of God will give the believers official reports or proclamations of "things to come" (John 16:13).

Appendix C

The Study of the 72 References to *Preaching* in the New Testament

Verse	What	By Whom	To Whom	Where
Matt. 12:41	Repentance	Jesus	Scribes/Pharisees	Outside
Luke 11:32	Repentance	Jesus	Scribes/Pharisees	Outside
Rom. 16:25	Gospel	Jesus	Church of Rome	Letter
1 Cor. 1:21; 2:4, 15:14	The cross of Christ (cross, death, resurrection)	"	Corinthians	Letter to Corinthians "
2 Tim. 4:17	The proclamation (the work of Jesus)	Paul	Gentiles	Not stated
Titus 1:3	The Word committed to Paul	Paul	Titus	Not stated (in Crete)
1 Tim. 2:7	Jesus Christ as ransom	Paul	Gentiles	Not stated
2 Tim. 1:11	Person/work/word of Jesus Christ	Paul	Gentiles	Not stated
2 Pet. 2:5	Preacher of righteousness; repentance	Noah	The ungodly	The ancient world

Verse	What	By Whom	To Whom	Where
Matt. 3:1	Kingdom of Heaven, repentance	John	In the wilderness	Judea
Matt. 4:17	Repent—Kingdom of Heaven	Jesus	General—unsaved	Region of Galilee
Matt. 4:23	The gospel of the Kingdom	Jesus	Jews and the sick people	Galilee synagogues
Matt. 9:35	Preaching and teaching the gospel of the Kingdom	Jesus	Jews—multitudes	Synagogue
Matt. 10:7	Kingdom of Heaven is at hand	The twelve disciples	House of Israel	Any town you enter
Matt. 10:27	The message	Jesus	Disciple	The housetops
Matt. 11:1	Teachings of Jesus	Jesus	City dwellers	Cities
Matt. 24:14, 26:13	The gospel of the Kingdom	Believers-disciples	Nations	World
Mark 1:4	Repentance	John	Unbelievers	Wilderness
Mark 1:7	Coming Messiah	John	Jews, unbelievers	Wilderness
Mark 1:14	Kingdom of God	Jesus	Jews, unbelievers	Galilee
Mark 1:38, 39	(Kingdom) preach	Christ	Jews	Neighboring towns
Mark 3:14	(Kingdom) preach	Disciples	To whomever, wherever they went	Synagogues throughout all Galilee
Mark 6:12	Repentance	Disciples	Men	Went out everywhere
Mark 14:9	Gospel	Anyone	Everyone	Whole world
Mark 16:15, 20	Gospel	Disciples	Everyone	Whole world
Luke 3:3	Baptism of repentance for remission	John	Everyone in the countries surrounding Jordan	All the country

Verse	What	By Whom	To Whom	Where
Luke 4:18, 19	The gospel; deliverance, the acceptable year of the Lord	Jesus	The poor	The synagogue
Luke 8:1	Kingdom of God	Jesus and the twelve	Those in the city and villages, certain women	Every city and village
Luke 9:2	Kingdom of God	Jesus—the twelve	To everyone	Sent everywhere
Luke 24:47	Repentance and remission of sins	Jesus—the disciples	All nations	All nations
Acts 8:5	The Word—Christ	Philip	People of Samaria	Samaria
Acts 9:20	To preach Christ	Saul	Jews	Synagogue
Acts 10:37	That word which was published throughout all Judea	Peter	Gentiles (house of Cornelius)	Caesarea
Acts 10:42	To preach and testify	Peter	Gentiles	House of Cornelius
Acts 15:21	Preach Christ (instruction)	James	Jews, Council of Jerusalem	Jerusalem
Acts 19:13	Jesus	Paul	To apparently everyone	Ephesus
Acts 20:25	Kingdom of God	Paul	Miletus	Elders of the church—Ephesus
Acts 28:31	Kingdom of God	Paul	Believers and unbelievers—all that came to his house	Paul's own house—Rome
Rom. 2:21	Proclaimed not to steal	Jews	To yourself and others	Rome
Rom. 10:8	Faith (Word)	We (Christians)	Jews	Rome
Rom. 10:15	Gospel of peace	They (believers)	To whosoever	Wherever they are sent out

Verse	What	By Whom	To Whom	Where
1 Cor. 1:23	Christ having been crucified	We (Paul and believers)	Jews and Greeks	Anywhere in the world
1 Cor. 9:27	The gospel	Paul	Preached to others	Anywhere
1 Cor. 15:11	The gospel	Paul	Corinthian church	Corinth
1 Cor. 15:12	Christ arose from the dead	Paul, the twelve, 500+	Corinthian church	Corinth
2 Cor. 1:19	The Son of God, Jesus Christ	Paul and others	The Corinthians	Around Corinth
2 Cor. 4:5	The gospel	Paul and others	Corinthians and all unbelievers	Corinth and the area
2 Cor. 11:4, 7	Another Jesus, another gospel	Someone other than Paul	The unsaved	Corinth and the area
Gal. 2:2	Gospel preached to the Gentiles	Paul	The Gentiles and then related to the leaders in Jerusalem	The Galatian area
Gal. 5:11	Circumcision as opposed to the offense of the cross	Paul	Unbelievers in the Galatian area	Galatian area
Phil. 1:15	Christ	Different ones	People in the palace	Various places
Col. 1:23	Hope of the gospel	Especially by Paul	Every creature	Everywhere
1 Thess. 2:9	Gospel of God	Paul and others	Thessalonians	Their area
1 Tim. 3:16	The work of Christ	Paul and others	The Gentiles	In the world
2 Tim. 4:2	The Word—Logos (John 1:1)	Timothy and others	Everyone	Everywhere
1 Pet. 3:19	The work of Christ (suffering of Christ for sin)	Christ	Spirits in prison	The place where they are held captive

Verse	What	By Whom	To Whom	Where
Mark 1:45	Life-changing power of Christ	Leper	All men	Abroad the city
Mark 5:20	" "	The demoniac	" "	" " "
Mark 7:36	" "	Deaf man	" "	" " "
Mark 13:10	The good news of Jesus	The disciples	" "	To the nations
Luke 8:39	Great things Jesus did	Devil-possessed man (saved)	Throughout the whole city (Gadarenes)	(City of unbelievers)
Luke 12:3	Beware of hypocrisy	Christ	Gathered multitude, but first to his disciples	Perea
Rev. 5:2	(The Word) who is worthy to open the book	Angel	In a vision	John (Isle of Patmos)
Mark 1:39	(Messiah)	Christ	Jews	Synagogues
Luke 4:44	Kingdom of God	Jesus	Galilee synagogue	(Unbelievers of Galilee)
Rom. 10:14	(Christ)	Paul—believers at Rome and everywhere	Unbelievers	Rome (everywhere)

Appendix D

Lecture XII,
The Kingly Office of Christ
By A. A. Hodge

This sermon by Dr. A. A. Hodge, "The Kingly Office of Christ" is reproduced here because less than fifty years after the establishment of the public schools (National Popular Education) Hodge in this sermon puts his finger on the problem of neutrality and predicts that public education will become "the most efficient and widespread instrument for the propagation of atheism that the world has ever seen."

In five pages toward the close of this sermon, Dr. Hodge gives us some of the best statements of rationale for the necessity of Christian education and the existence of the Christian school. You will not only be blessed by his sermon, but stirred by his prophetic educational insight.

There are not two laws for individuals and for communities. The obligations which bind individuals necessarily bind all the communities which these individuals constitute. Every human being is bound to be Christian; therefore every community of human beings is bound to obey the law of Christ. The United States, as a matter of historic fact, have always professed to be a Christian State, and we are therefore doubly bound to this allegiance—(1) by virtue of the common obligation which binds all men; (2) by virtue of the special opportunities and covenants of our ancestors, which descend upon us by natural inheritance.

V. The overwhelming importance of this principle and weight of this obligation appear in the clearest light the moment the nation claims to regulate the supreme function of education. It is insisted upon that the right of self-preservation is the highest law of States as well as of individuals; that if the suffrage is universal, all holders of that suffrage must be educated in order to secure the safety of the State; that in consequence of the heterogeneous character of our population and the divisions of the Christian Church there is no agency in existence competent to educate the whole body of the holders of the universal suffrage except the State herself.

The situation, therefore, stands thus:

1st. The tendency of the entire system, in which already vast progress has been made, is to centralization. Each State governs her own system of common schools by a central agency, which brings them, for the sake of greater efficiency, into uniformity of method and rules. These schools are graded and supplemented by normal schools, high schools and crowned by the State university. The tendency is to unite all these school systems of the several States in one uniform national system, providing with all the abundant resources of the nation for the entire education of its citizens in every department of human knowledge, and in doing this to establish a uniform curriculum of study, uniform standards for the selection of teachers and a uniform school literary apparatus of textbooks, etc.

2d. The tendency is to hold that this system must be altogether secular. The atheistic doctrine is gaining currency, even among professed Christians and even among some bewildered Christian ministers, that an education provided by the common government for the children of diverse religious parties should be entirely emptied of all religious character. The Protestants object to the government schools being used for the purpose of inculcating the doctrines of the Catholic Church, and Romanists object to the use of the Protestant version of the Bible and to the inculcation of the peculiar doctrines of the Protestant churches. The Jews protest against the schools being used to inculcate Christianity in any form, and the atheists and agnostics protest against any teaching that implies the existence and moral government of God. It is capable of exact demonstration that if every party in the State has the right of excluding from the public schools whatever he does not believe to be true, then he that believes most must give way to him that believes least, and then he that believes least must give way to him that believes absolutely nothing, no matter in how small a minority the atheists or the agnostics may be. It is self-evident that on this scheme, if it is consistently and persistently carried out in all parts of the country, the United States system of national popular education will be the most efficient and wide instrument for the propagation of Atheism which the world has ever seen.

3d. The claim of impartiality between positions as directly contradictory as that of Jews, Mohammedans and Christians, and especially as that of theists and of atheists, is evidently absurd. And no less is the claim absurd and impossible that a system of education can be indifferent on these fundamental subjects. There is no possible branch of human knowledge which is not purely formal, like abstract logic or mathematics, which can be known or taught in a spirit of entire indifferency between Theism and Atheism. Every department which deals with realities, either principles, objective things or substances, or with events, must be in reality one or the other; if it be not positively and confessedly theistic, it must be really and in full effect atheistic. The physical as well as the moral universe must be conceived either in a theistic or an atheistic light. It must originate in and develop through intelligent will—that is, in a person—or in atoms, force or chance. Teleology must be acknowledged everywhere or be denied everywhere. Philosophy, ethics, jurisprudence, political and social science can be conceived of and treated only from a theistic or from an atheistic point of view. The proposal to treat them from a neutral point of view is ignorant and absurd. English common law is unintelligible if not read in the light of that religion in which it had its genesis. The English language cannot be sympathetically understood or taught by a mind blind to the everywhere-present current of religious thought and life which expresses itself through its terms. The history of Christendom, especially the history of the English-speaking races, and the philosophy of history in general, will prove an utterly insoluble riddle to all who attempt to read it in any nontheistic, religiously-indifferent sense. It is certain that throughout the entire range of the higher education a position of entire indifferentism is an absolute impossibility— that along the entire line the relation of man and of the universe to the ever-present God, the supreme Lord of the conscience and heart, the nonaffirmation of the truth, is entirely equivalent to the affirmation at every point of its opposite.

The prevalent superstition that men can be educated for good citizenship or for any other use under heaven without religion is as unscientific and unphilosophical as it is irreligious. It deliberately leaves out of view the most essential and controlling elements of human character: that man is constitutionally as religious (*i.e.* loyally or disloyally) as he is rational; that morals are impossible when dissociated from the religious basis out of which they grow; that, as a matter of fact, human liberty and stable republican institutions, and every practically successful scheme of universal education in all past history, have originated in the active ministries of the Christian religion, and in these alone. This miserable superstition rests upon no facts of experience, and, on the contrary, is maintained on purely theoretical grounds in opposition to all the lessons which the past history of our race furnishes on the subject.

It is no answer to say that the deficiency of the national system of education in this regard will be adequately supplied by the activities of the Christian churches. No court would admit in excuse for the diffusion of poison the plea that the poisoner knew of another agent actively employed in diffusing an antidote. Moreover, the churches, divided and without national recognition, would be able very inadequately to counteract the deadly evil done by the public schools of the State with all the resources and prestige of the government. But, more than all, Atheism taught in the school cannot be counteracted by Theism taught in the Church. Theism and Atheism cannot coalesce to make anything. All truth in all spheres is organically one and vitally inseparable. It is impossible for different agencies independently to discuss and inculcate the religious and the purely naturalistic sides of truth respectively. They cannot be separated; in some degree they must recognize each other and be taught together, as they are experienced in their natural relations.

I am as sure as I am of the fact of Christ's reign that a comprehensive and centralized system of national education, separated from religion, as is now commonly proposed, will prove the most appalling enginery for the propagation of anti-Christian and atheistic unbelief, and of antisocial nihilistic ethics, individual, social and political, which this sin-rent world has ever seen.

Appendix E
The Bible and Culture

The transmission of any message can never be separated from culture. The Bible likewise, as a message from God, is completely and totally couched in the framework of culture. Therefore, the Bible is totally communicated to us within the context of culture, but it is not culturally limited. The Bible stands above culture, and therefore is not limited by it.

How is the Bible supra-, trans-, or cross-cultural? Our analysis must be historical and grammatical. This probably could be called the cultural (historical) grammatical approach. The passage must be understood in the historical, that is, cultural setting; however, only the concept or principle(s) are supra-, trans-, or cross-cultural. An inspired (God-exhaled) authoritative, inerrant text has carefully given to us the details of information (facts) in a specific cultural setting in order to insure the accuracy of the Bible doctrines or concepts which now in principle may be universally applied.

If the Bible is culturally communicated, then how can the

Bible not be culturally limited? Using culture—that is, language
and life-styles—God has communicated to us concepts or basic
principles to provide for us the guidelines upon which we are
able to build our patterns, structures, and forms. It is the position of the writer that the Bible nowhere gives to us the structures or forms, but consistently communicates to us basic foundational principles or concepts. Even in relationship to such
matters as the Lord's table (1 Corinthians 11), the Scripture is
not giving to us the actual form or structure involved, but is
simply communicating to us a series of principles or concepts
which provide for us, as Francis Schaeffer would say, a shadow
of the actual form or structure that is involved.

Therefore, the Bible nowhere gives to us complete patterns, structures, or forms in relationship to what we are sup-
posed to be doing, but conveys to us the concepts which help us
develop the principles. These we apply to each individual culture to produce the form suitable for that culture.

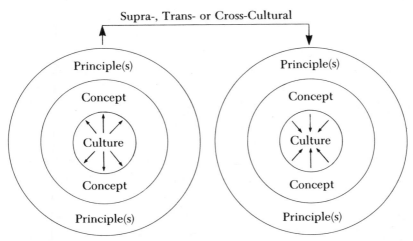

The Bible, given to us in a cultural setting by means of a cultural
framework (language, illustrations, and so on), has conveyed to us all the
facts or bits of information which form the concepts. From the concepts,
the facts brought together into a meaningful relationship, we can discern
the principle(s) which then become supra-, trans- or cross-cultural. The
principles are then applied to help us regain the true perspective of the
concept, and this is then applied to the contemporary culture. Thus a Bible
that gives to us principles and does not lock us into cultural structures can
always, at any time, be culturally applicable.

How then do we arrive at the principles that the Bible conveys to us? Obviously all the things that are directly commanded must be followed or applied but in principle, not necessarily in the exact pattern or form in which they were culturally communicated. The hermeneutic that would be used for determining other matters not directly commanded in Scripture would be: those things which are repeated again and again provide for us the concept which enables us to establish a principle and ultimately a norm for present-day church practice. Thus, even though the Bible is culturally communicated, and culture involves form and structure, because the Bible is supra-cultural, the focus of attention is not on the culture, the pattern or form, but on the concepts and principles being conveyed to us.

The following may serve to illustrate the application of the approach previously described. Nowhere in the New Testament is there a specific command to meet on the first day of the week. However, consistently again and again the emphasis of the New Testament is that they met on the first day of the week and, in fact, no other specific day is consistently mentioned. Thus, with the application of the hermeneutic, the concept or principle would be that the church regularly met on the first day of the week. Thus in this case there was a sharp break with culture by changing from meeting on the Sabbath to meeting on Sunday, or the first day of the week.

This same approach can be applied in additional areas such as (1) the term *elder* is never used in the singular in relationship to a specific local church; (2) with the seventy-two references to the word *preach,* only a few of them refer to preaching actually being done in the church when the believers are gathered together; (3) we find no commands for the lost to come to church to find Christ, but multiplied commands for the believer to take the message of the gospel to the lost where they are; (4) greet one another with a holy kiss; (5) we see repetition of the concept "build up one another."

How Do You Determine

Absolutes	*Nonabsolutes*
Principles	Patterns
Function	Forms
Directives	Means
Purpose	Methods
Objectives	Structures
WHY?	HOW?

WHAT?

To reiterate, those things that consistently appear give to us the concept which may actually be the principle or help us to develop the principle from which we are able to develop the norm and ultimately the form or pattern.

Appendix F

Church Leadership in the New Testament—Use of the Word Elder

DATA	Pastor(s)?			Number		Indi-vidual	Church		
	Yes	?	No	Sg.	Pl		Sg.	?	Pl
(Old Testament and gospel instances are not included because they cannot refer to the N.T. Church).									
Pastors									
Eph. 4:11	√				√	√			
Elders									
Luke 15:25			√						
1 Timothy 5:1			√						
2			√						
19	√			√		√			
1 Peter 5:5	√			√		√			
2 John 1		√							
3 John 1		√							
Acts 4:5			√						
8			√						
Acts 4:23			√						
6:12			√						
11:30	√				√			*Judea* √	
14:23	√				√		√		
15:2	√				√		√		
4	√				√		√		
6	√				√		√		
22	√				√		√		
23	√				√		√		
16:4	√				√		√		
20:17	√				√		√		
21:18	√				√		√		
23:14			√						
24:1			√						

	A	B	C	D	E	F	G	H
25:15		√						
1 Tim. 5:17	√			√	√			
Titus 1:5	√			√			City √	
Hebrews 11:2		√						
James 5:14	√			√		√		
1 Peter 5:1	√			√				√

(Revelation instances are also omitted, as they each refer to paradise, not the church on earth).

(Elder)

	A	B	C	D	E	F	G	H
Acts 22:5		√						
Rom. 9:12		√						
1 Peter 5:1	√		√		√			

(Bishop)

	A	B	C	D	E	F	G	H
1 Tim. 3:1	√		√		√			
Acts 1:20		√						
1 Tim. 3:2	√		√		√			
Titus 1:7	√		√		√			
1 Peter 2:25							Saints √	
Phil. 1:1	√			√				

Church Leadership Mentioned Twenty-two Times

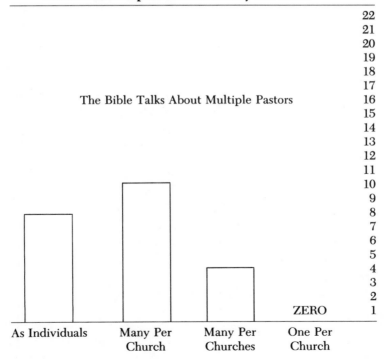

The Bible Talks About Multiple Pastors

As Individuals	Many Per Church	Many Per Churches	One Per Church
			ZERO

Appendix G

Questions to Stimulate Your Thinking in the Basic Areas of Christian Education

Basic Areas

               traditional—Herbart

I.   Philosophy   —Comenius

               progressive—Dewey

II. Principles   biblical

                  educational

                  organizational and administrational

III. Procedure for Implementation

IV. Program

V. Problems

VI. Projection—trends

VII. Publications

Questions:

I. Philosophy

1. Develop your personal philosophy of Christian education showing its implications in relationship to your philosophy of the ministry. Include such things as theological principles (the written Word and the Holy Spirit), your basic assumptions as well as what you feel are the distinctive qualities and the implications of your personal philosophy of Christian education.

2. Believing that not only what Jesus Christ said, but also what He did as recorded in the Word of God is completely inspired, evaluate what the Gospels give to us regarding the educational philosophy of Jesus Christ.

3. Is Jesus Christ called the "Master-Teacher" simply because He is the Son of God and therefore is the God-man, or is there a sound educational rationale for this unique designation?

4. Because as Christians we hold to the fixed revelation of the Word, is there a place for Christian educators to experience true academic freedom? The world of education is making a great deal of the concept of academic freedom today, and as Christian educators we need to understand the place and relevance of this concept in the field of Christian education.

II. Principles

1. What are the key biblical passages which are relevant to Christian education? Include the passages of Scripture pertinent to the ministry of Christian education and the educational implications found in these verses or passages of Scripture.

2. In addition to the area of teaching methodology, what beyond this specifically adds strength to Christian education?

3. Discuss the biblical as well as the educational basis or justification for organization and administration.

4. Discuss the principles pertaining to the teaching-learning process.

III. Procedures

1. Define *leadership* and discuss the role of the leader in the program of the local church.
2. Define *curriculum* and demonstrate its place in the program of Christian education. In addition, discuss some of the practical problems, particularly in relationship to developing a curriculum consistent with our Christian philosophy of education.
3. As a director of Christian education, you will always be in a church as a part of a multiple-staff situation. What should be the working relationship, not only to the pastor, but to any additional members of the staff?
4. Discuss the concept of team teaching in relationship to the open concept of education, showing the particular contribution it can make in Christian education.

IV. Program

1. Discuss both biblically and practically the program or ministry of evangelism in relationship to the ministry of the local church.
2. Briefly trace the historical development of the Sunday-school movement, particularly focusing on the present-day trend or trends in relationship to this church agency.

V. Problems

1. Integration in Christian education has been referred to as the missing ingredient. Discuss the problem of integration in Christian education as it relates to Truth with truth and ultimately with life.
2. Someone has said that the greatest unresolved problem in the local church is a lack of leadership. Do you concur with

this evaluation, and if so, what do you see as the biblical and practical reasons for the problem? What solution or solutions would you propose?

VI. Projections-Trends

1. Recently, I was told that all Christian education would eventually be done in the local church by professional teachers (not necessarily paid). How do you react to this?
2. Relate what you consider to be significant trends in Christian education (local church, camping, Christian school).

VII. Publications (Books and Periodicals)

See Bibliography.

Source Notes

Chapter 1

1. Paul Monroe, ed., "Education," *A Cyclopedia of Education*, vol. 2 (New York: Macmillan, 1911), p. 400.
2. John Dewey, *Democracy and Education* (New York: Free Press, 1966), pp. 89, 90.
3. Ibid., p. 126.
4. Monroe, "Education," p. 398.
5. Bernard Iddings Bell, *Crisis in Education* (New York: McGraw-Hill, 1949), p. 57.
6. Harry S. Broudy, *Building a Philosophy of Education* (New York: Prentice-Hall, 1954), p. 9.
7. John Milburn Price et al., *A Survey of Religious Education* (New York: Ronald Press, 1940), pp. 13, 14.
8. "Philosophy and Practice of Education" *The Volume Library* (New York: Educators Association, Inc., 1953), p. 17.
9. Ibid.
10. Theodore J. Jansma, *What Is Christian Education?* (Chicago: National Association of Christian Schools, n.d.), p. 1.
11. Ibid.
12. Gerald F. Ensley, *The Marks of Christian Education* (New York: Methodist Pub. House, 1958), p. 15.
13. Ibid., p. 14.
14. Roy Zuck, *Spiritual Power in Your Teaching* (Chicago: Moody Press, 1972), p. 9.
15. Earle E. Cairns, "The Essence of Christian Higher Education," *Bibliotheca Sacra* 110 (October 1954): 343.
16. Ibid., p. 341.

Chapter 3

1. Roger Lincoln Shinn, *Christianity and the Problem of History* (New York: Charles Scribner's Sons, 1953), p. 13.
2. Mark Fakkema, *Christian Philosophy* Christian Philosophy of Education and Its Implications, vol. 1 (Wheaton, Ill.: National Association of Christian Schools, 1952), p. 2.
3. Ibid., p. 85.

4. Ibid.
5. *Webster's New International Dictionary of the English Language, Unabridged,* 2nd ed. (Springfield, Mass.: G & C Merriam, 1960), p. 1842.
6. Lois Emogene LeBar, *Education That Is Christian* (Westwood, N.J.: Fleming H. Revell Co., 1958), p. 205.
7. Gordon H. Clark, *A Christian Philosophy of Education* (Grand Rapids, Mich.: Wm. B. Eerdmans, 1946), pp. 40, 41.

Chapter 4

1. Frank E. Gaebelein, *The Pattern of God's Truth* (Chicago: Moody Press, 1968), p. 9.
2. Ibid., p. 11.
3. Ibid., p. 15.
4. Gordon H. Clark, *A Christian Philosophy of Education* (Grand Rapids, Mich.: Wm. B. Eerdmans, 1946), pp. 208–210.
5. Edwin H. Rian, *Christianity and American Education* (San Antonio: Naylor Co., 1949), p. 236.
6. Charles Ryrie, *Biblical Theology of the New Testament* (Chicago: Moody Press, 1959), p. 12.
7. Ibid.
8. Ibid., p. 22.
9. Ibid., p. 23.
10. Frank L. Ryan, *Exemplars for the New Social Studies: Instruction in the Elementary Schools* (Englewood Cliffs, N.J.: Prentice-Hall, 1971), p. 15.
11. Ralph Tyler, *Basic Principles of Curriculum and Instruction.* (Chicago: University of Chicago Press, 1969), pp. 89–94.
12. Ibid., pp. 94, 95.
13. Jonathan C. McLendon, *Social Studies in Secondary Education* (New York: Macmillan Co., 1965), pp. 3–9.
14. Tyler, pp. 76, 77.

Chapter 5

1. LeBar, p. 206.
2. Othanel Smith, William O. Stanley, and J. Harlan Shores, *Fundamentals of Curriculum Development,* rev. ed. (New York: Harcourt, Brace, and World, Inc., 1957), p. 3.
3. LeBar, p. 203.
4. Ibid.
5. Tyler, p. 1.
6. Lewis B. Mayhew, *Contemporary College Students and the Curriculum* (Atlanta: Southern Regional Ed. Bd, 1969), p. 33.

Chapter 6

1. Clark, p. 76.
2. Ibid.
3. A. A. Hodge, *Popular Lectures on Theological Themes* (Philadelphia, Pa.: Presbyterian Board of Publication, 1887), p. 281.
4. Clark, p. 76.
5. Ibid., p. 77.
6. Ibid.
7. Ibid.
8. Ibid., p. 79.
9. Hodge, p. 282.
10. Ibid., p. 283.
11. Ibid., p. 282.
12. T. Robert Ingram, "Education and Faith: A Plea for Christian Day Schools," *Christianity Today,* August 27, 1961, p. 3.
13. "Bible Banned," *The Prairie Overcomer,* June 1961, p. 205.
14. *See* Hodge, pp. 280, 281 for further discussion.
15. Clark, pp. 79, 80.
16. Ibid., p. 144.
17. Hodge, pp. 283, 284.
18. Gaebelein, p. 20.
19. Luella Cole, *A History of Education: Socrates to Montessori* (New York: Rinehart and Company, 1950), p. 618.
20. The Delaware County Christian School, *The Delaware County Christian School Manual* (Newton Square, Pa.: The Delaware County Christian School, n.d.), p. 3.
21. Roy W. Lowrie, Jr., "Christian School Administration," *The Christian Teacher* 110 (May 1960), p. 7.
22. Wheaton Christian Grammar School, *Wheaton Christian Grammar School Catalog* (Wheaton, Ill.: Wheaton Christian Grammar School, 1980).
23. Statement by Roy W. Lowrie, Jr. in a personal interview, May 1961.
24. Ibid.
25. Statement by Roy W. Lowrie, Jr. in a personal letter, October 1961.
26. LeBar, p. 20.
27. Clark, p. 192.

Chapter 7

1. "Down With All Truism," *Time* (February 1960).
2. *The World Almanac and Book of Facts* (New York: Newspaper Enterprise Association, Inc., 1980), p. 734.
3. *Encyclopaedia Britannica Book of the Year* (Chicago: Encyclopaedia Britannica, Inc., 1979).

4. Earl O. Radmacher, *What the Church Is All About* (Chicago: Moody
    Press, 1978), pp. 115, 130.
5. Robert L. Saucy, *The Church in God's Program* (Chicago: Moody
    Press, 1972), p. 16.
6. Leon J. Wood, *The Holy Spirit in the Old Testament* (Grand Rapids,
    Mich.: Zondervan, 1976), p. 74.
7. New Testament: Matthew 28:1; Mark 16:2, 9; Luke 24:1; John 20:1,
    19; Acts 20:7; 1 Corinthians 16:2. There is one reference to the Lord's
    Day: Revelation 1:10.
8. Francis A. Schaeffer, *The Church at the End of the Twentieth Century*
    (Wheaton, Ill: Inter-Varsity Press, 1970), p. 63.
9. *See* Appendix F.
10. F. F. Bruce, *The Books of Acts*, The New International Commentary
    on the New Testament (Grand Rapids, Mich.: Wm. B. Eerdmans,
    1954), p. 77.

Chapter 8

1. Diana Baumrind, "Current Patterns of Parental Authority," *Develop-
    mental Psychology Monographs* 4 (1971): pp. 99–103.
2. Archibald T. Robertson, *Grammar of the Greek New Testament in the
    Light of Historical Research* (Nashville, Tenn.: Broadman, 1947), p. 946.
3. James Orr, *International Standard Bible Encyclopedia*, vol. 2 rev. ed.
    (Grand Rapids, Mich.: Wm. B. Eerdmans, 1930), p. 851.
4. Ibid.
5. Bill Crouch, "Africa Now," *Sudan Interior Mission* (Sept.–Oct. 1973),
    p. 3.
6. Lawrence O. Richards, *Creative Bible Teaching* (Chicago: Moody Press,
    1970), p. 75.
7. George Peters, *A Biblical Theology of Missions* (Chicago: Moody Press,
    1972), p. 172.
8. John Milburn Price et al., *Jesus the Teacher* (Nashville, Tenn.: Sunday
    School Board of the Southern Baptist Convention, 1946), pp. 6, 7.
9. *See* Galatians 4:6: the Spirit of Christ and the Holy Spirit are the same.

Chapter 9

1. Charles Silberman, *Crisis in the Classroom: The Remaking of American
    Education* (New York: Vintage Books, 1970), p. 472.
2. Hodge, pp. 280, 281.
3. Clark, pp. 79, 80.
4. Hodge, pp. 280, 281.

Chapter 10

1.   Silberman, p. 472.

Chapter 11

1.   Dr. Daniel Noonan, "Drug Interactions With Alcohol," cassette, series 400–6, 1972.
2.   Ibid.
3.   Price, *Jesus the Teacher*, p. 2.

Bibliography

Association for the Advancement of Christian Scholarship. *To Prod the "Slumbering Giant."* Ontario, Canada: Wedge Publishing Foundation, 1972.

Bell, Bernard Iddings. *Crisis in Education.* New York: McGraw-Hill, 1949.

Beversluis, N. H. *Christian Philosophy of Education.* Grand Rapids, Mich.: National Union of Christian Schools, 1971.

Blamires, Harry. *The Christian Mind.* New York: Seabury Press, 1963.

Bloom, Benjamin S., and Krathwohl, D. R. *Taxonomy of Educational Objectives, Handbook I: Cognitive Domain.* New York: Longmans Green & Co., 1956.

Broudy, Harry S. *Building a Philosophy of Education.* New York: Prentice-Hall, 1954.

Brubacher, John S. *Modern Philosophies of Education.* 2d ed. New York: McGraw-Hill, 1950.

Bruner, Jerome S. *The Process of Education.* Cambridge, Mass.: Harvard University Press, 1960.

Bushnell, Horace. *Christian Nurture.* Grand Rapids, Mich.: Baker Book House, 1979.

Butler, J. Donald. *Religious Education: The Foundation and Practice of Nurture.* New York: Harper & Row, 1962.

Byrne, Herbert W. *A Christian Approach to Education: Educational Theory and Application.* rev. ed. Milford, Mich.: Mott Media, 1977.

Cantor, Nathaniel. *The Teaching-Learning Process.* New York: Henry Holt, 1953.

Clark, Gordon H. *A Christian Philosophy of Education.* Grand Rapids, Mich.: Wm. B. Eerdmans, 1946.

Cole, Luella. *A History of Education: Socrates to Montessori.* New York: Rinehart and Company, 1950.

Comenius, John Ames. *The Great Didactic.* London: A & C Black, 1910.

Cubberly, Elwood P. *The History of Education.* Boston: Houghton Mifflin, 1922.

Cully, Kendig Brubaker, *Basic Writings in Christian Education.* Philadelphia: Westminster Press, 1960.

Deighton, Lee C., ed. *The Encyclopedia of Education.* 10 vols. New York: Macmillan, 1971.

The Delaware County Christian School. *The Delaware County Christian School Manual.* Newton Square, Pa.: The Delaware County Christian School, n.d.

Dewey, John. *The Child and the Curriculum and the School and Society.* 2d ed. Chicago: University of Chicago Press, 1956.

Dewey, John. *Democracy and Education.* New York: Free Press, 1966.

Dewey, John. *Experience and Education.* New York: Macmillan, 1963.

Dewey, John. *Reconstruction in Philosophy.* New York: Henry Holt and Company, 1920.

DeJong, Jerome Bernard. "The Parent Controlled Christian School." Ph.D. dissertation, New York University, 1954.

DeYong, Chris A. *Introduction to American Public Education.* 3d ed. New York: McGraw-Hill, 1955.

Dobson, James. *Dare to Discipline.* Wheaton, Ill.: Tyndale House, 1971.

Dobson, James. *Hide or Seek.* Old Tappan, N.J.: Fleming H. Revell, 1974.

Eby, Arrowood, and Flinn, Charles. *The History of Philosophy of Education: Ancient and Medieval.* New York: Prentice-Hall, 1940.

Edge, Findley B. *Teaching for Results.* Nashville, Tenn.: Broadman Press, 1956.

Fakkema, Mark. *Christian Philosophy.* Christian Philosophy of Education and Its Implications, vol. 1. Wheaton, Ill.: National Association of Christian Schools, 1952.

Fakkema, Mark. *Moral Discipline.* Christian Philosophy of Education and Its Implications, vol. 2. Wheaton, Ill.: National Association of Christian Schools, 1953.

Fakkema, Mark. *Christian Teaching.* Christian Philosophy of Education and Its Implication, vol. 3. Wheaton, Ill.: National Association of Christian Schools, 1954.

Fallow, Wesner. *Christian Education for Tomorrow.* Philadelphia, Pa.: Westminster Press, 1960.

Fennema, Jack. *Nurturing Children in the Lord.* Phillipsburg, N.J.: Presbyterian and Reformed Publishing, 1978.

Ford, Leroy. *A Primer for Teachers and Leaders.* Nashville, Tenn.: Broadman Press, 1963.

Gaebelein, Frank E. *Christian Education in a Democracy.* New York: Oxford University Press, 1951.

Gaebelein, Frank E. *The Pattern of God's Truth.* Chicago: Moody Press, 1968.

Gangel, Kenneth O. *Twenty-four Ways to Improve Your Teaching.* Wheaton, Ill.: Victor Books.

Getz, Gene A. *Sharpening the Focus of the Church.* Chicago: Moody Press, 1976.

Good, Carter V., ed. *Dictionary of Education.* New York: McGraw-Hill, 1959.

Gregory, Milton. *Seven Laws of Teaching.* Grand Rapids, Mich.: Baker Book House, 1972.

Griffin, E. M. *The Mind Changers.* Wheaton, Ill.: Tyndale House, 1976.

Hegland, Martin. *Christianity in Education.* Minneapolis, Minn.: Augsburg, 1954.

Hodge, A. A. *Popular Lectures on Theological Themes.* Philadelphia, Pa.: Presbyterian Board of Publication, 1887.

Holmes, Arthur. *All Truth Is God's Truth,* Grand Rapids, Mich.: Wm. B. Eerdmans, 1977.

Hook, Sidney. *Education for Modern Man.* New York: Dial Press, 1946.

Horne, Herman Harrell. *The Democratic Philosophy of Education.* New York: Macmillan, 1932.

Horne, Herman Harrell. *Teaching Techniques of Jesus.* Grand Rapids, Mich.: Kregel Publications, 1971.

Horne, Herman Harrell. *The Philosophy of Christian Education.* New York: Fleming H. Revell, 1937.

Jaarsma, Cornelius. *Fundamentals in Christian Education.* Grand Rapids, Mich.: Wm. B. Eerdmans, 1953.

Jansma, Theodore J. *What Is Christian Education?* Chicago: National Association of Christian Schools, n.d.

Kienel, Paul A. *The Christian School: Why It Is Right for Your Child.* Wheaton, Ill.: Victor Books, 1974.

Kienel, Paul A. *The Philosophy of Christian School Education.* Whittier, Cal.: Western Association, 1977.

Kilpatrick, William Heard. *The Philosophy of Education.* New York: Macmillan, 1936.

Knight, Edgar Wallace, *Fifty Years of American Education 1900–1950.* New York: Ronald Press, 1952.

Krathwohl, David, et al. *Affective Domain.* Taxonomy of Educational Objectives, vol 2. New York: Longman, Inc., 1964.

LeBar, Lois Emogene. *Education That Is Christian.* Westwood, N.J.: Fleming H. Revell, 1958.

Le Fevre, Perry Deyo. *The Christian Teacher.* Nashville, Tenn.: Abingdon Press, 1958.

Lockerbie, D. Bruce. *The Way They Should Go.* New York: Oxford University Press, 1972.

Lowrie, Roy W., Jr. *Inside the Christian School.* Whittier, Cal.: Association of Christian Schools International, 1980.

Lowrie, Roy W., Jr. *To Those Who Teach in Christian Schools.* Whittier, Cal.: Association of Christian Schools International, 1978.

May, Philip. *Which Way to Educate?* Chicago: Moody Press, 1975.

Mayhew, Lewis B., and Ford, Patrick J. *Changing the Curriculum.* San Francisco: Jossey-Bass, 1971.

Miller, Randolph Crump. *Education for Christian Living.* Englewood Cliffs, N.J.: Prentice-Hall, 1956.

Monroe, Paul, ed. *A Cyclopedia of Education.* 5 vols. New York: Macmillan, 1911.

Murch, James DeForest. *Teach or Perish.* Grand Rapids, Mich.: Wm. B. Eerdmans, 1961.

Mursell, James L. *Developmental Teaching.* New York: McGraw-Hill, 1949.

Nazigian, Arthur. *Teach Them Diligently*. Brookhaven, Pa.: The Christian Academy, 1974.

Oppewal, Donald. *Roots of the Calvanistic Day School Movement*. Grand Rapids, Mich.: The Calvin College Monograph.

Price, John Milburn et al. *A Survey of Religious Education*. New York: Ronald Press, 1940.

Price, John Milburn et al. *Jesus the Teacher*. Nashville, Tenn.: Sunday School Board of the Southern Baptist Convention, 1946.

Ramm, Bernard. *The Christian View of Science and Scripture*. Grand Rapids, Mich.: Wm. B. Eerdmans, 1954.

Ramsay, William Mitchell. *Education of Christ*. London: Hodder and Stoughton, 1902.

Richards, Lawrence O. *Creative Bible Teaching*. Chicago: Moody Press, 1970.

Richards, Lawrence O. *A New Face for the Church*. Grand Rapids, Mich.: Zondervan, 1978.

Richards, Lawrence O. *A Theology of Christian Education*. Grand Rapids, Mich.: Zondervan, 1975.

Rushdoony, Rousas J. *Intellectual Schizophrenia*. Phillipsburg, N.J.: Presbyterian and Reformed Pub., n.d.

Rushdoony, Rousas J. *Messianic Character of American Education*. Phillipsburg, N.J.: Presbyterian and Reformed Pub., n.d.

Ryan, Frank L. *Exemplars for the New Social Studies: Instruction in the Elementary Schools*. Englewood Cliffs, N.J.: Prentice-Hall, 1971.

Saucy, Robert L. *The Church in God's Program*. Chicago: Moody Press, 1972.

Seerveld, Calvin. *Cultural Objectives for the Christian Teacher*. Palos Heights, Ill.: Trinity Christian College.

Sherrill, Lewis Joseph. *The Rise of Christian Education*. New York: Macmillan, 1944.

Shinn, Roger Lincoln. *Christianity and the Problem of History*. New York: Charles Scribner's Sons, 1953.

Silberman, Charles E. *Crisis in the Classroom: The Remaking of American Education*. New York: Vintage Books, 1970.

Simpson, Frances. "The Development of the National Association of Christian Schools." Ph.D. dissertation, Southwestern Baptist Theological Seminary, 1955.

Steensma, Geraldine, ed. *Shaping School Curriculum*. Terre Haute, Ind.: Signal Publishing Consulting Corp., 1977.

Steensma, Geraldine. *To Those Who Teach*. Signal Mountain, Tenn.: Signal Publishing Consulting Corp., 1971.

Taylor, M. J. *Religious Education: A Comprehensive Survey*. Nashville, Tenn.: Abingdon, 1960.

Thayer, V. T. *Religion in Public Education*. New York: Viking Press, 1947.

Tyler, Ralph. *Basic Principles of Curriculum and Instruction*. Chicago: University of Chicago Press, 1969.

Van Der Kooy, T. *The Distinctive Features of the Christian School.* Grand Rapids, Mich.: Wm. B. Eerdmans, 1925.

Van Dusen, Henry P. *God in Education.* New York: Charles Scribner's Sons, 1951.

Volume Library. New York: Educators Association, Inc., 1953.

Van Til, Cornelius. *The Dilemma of Education.* 2d rev. ed. Philadelphia, Pa.: Presbyterian and Reformed Pub., 1956.

Waterink, Jan. *Basic Concepts in Christian Pedagogy.* Grand Rapids, Mich.: Wm. B. Eerdmans, 1954.

Webster's New Collegiate Dictionary. Springfield, Mass.: G & C Merriam, 1973.

Webster's New International Dictionary of the English Language, Unabridged. 2d ed. Springfield, Mass.: G & C Merriam, 1960.

Worrell, Edward A. *Restoring God to Education.* Wheaton, Ill.: Van Kampen Press, 1950.

Wykoff, D. Campbell. *Theory and Design of Christian Education Curriculum.* Philadelphia, Pa.: Westminster Press, 1972.

Zuck, Roy B. *Spiritual Power in Your Teaching.* Chicago: Moody Press, 1972.

Index